L. Sydney Fisher

"I learned at a very early age that two things and two things alone protect America from those who seek to destroy it - The grace of Almighty God & the United States Military."

~ Charlie Daniels

MORE BY L. SYDNEY FISHER

Dedicated with admiration and respect to the men and women of the United States Military. Past, present, and future.

To the men and women serving in any and all law enforcement agencies of federal, state, and local jurisdiction who protect our homeland.

I salute you.

And dedicated with love to...

BRYCE, my star child

Editing provided by: Kathleen Hillman McCormick

PAPERBACK EDITION
ISBN-13: 978-1545256244
ISBN-10: 1545256241

Cover Design: L. Sydney Fisher

Introduction with Acknowledgments

During the 1990's, the United States Army trained special agents believed to hold extraordinary supernatural abilities. The secret program known as Star Gate used a method of psychic spying or remote viewing to see beyond normal human ability. Remote viewing is a term coined by the military but is otherwise known as clairvoyance. Although this program was shut down in November 1995 after a CIA investigation deemed it non-contributory to the military, I believe the project was worth the research, but our ability to harness the power behind telekinesis was too far into the future for our current understanding.

A couple of years ago, I stumbled across a book by Major Ed Dames and Joel Harry Newman titled *Tell Me What You See*. The book was Dames' personal account as an operations and training officer for the Defense Intelligence Agency's Psychic Intelligence Unit. Within seconds of thumbing through the pages, I found myself hooked. Suddenly, years of my own curiosities and personal experiences were validated, and I became totally consumed with learning all about the military's interest in Parapsychology, the same subject that I had spent my entire life researching while struggling to convince myself that my own psychic experiences were definitely real and not the result of an overactive imagination. My fascination with Star Gate prompted a year's worth of investigations. I studied numerous articles and books related to the Army's remote viewing program, telekinesis, telepathy, and clairvoyance. And I have included a suggested reading list, a few of my favorites, at the end of this book for those of you who want to explore the subject.

During the months that followed Seth Phoenix's transformation from the creative recesses of my mind to the pages that followed, I sought the help of military personnel and soldiers willing to give me an interview and a look inside their world. And with deep appreciation, I acknowledge and thank these individuals.

To Deputy Joshua Hood, former sergeant in the U. S. Army 82nd Airborne and author of the Mason Kane series and debut novel, Clear by Fire (Simon and Schuster) …thank you for sharing your knowledge and giving me your time. During the months that followed, you were always "just a phone call away" if I needed your help. I will always appreciate your friendship and admire your undeniable talent as an author.

To Ret. Command Sergeant Major Ronald V. Coleman, your leadership and knowledge were invaluable to my research and proved to be the key I needed in creating Seth Phoenix. I offer my sincerest gratitude.

To Lieutenant Colonel Kelly Mims, U. S. Army Reserve, who has probably already forgotten about this project… thank you for your time and knowledge all those months ago, when I first began building the outline and foundation for The Phoenix Mission.

To my readers… within these pages, you will find historical fiction interwoven with a little science fiction and a dose of reality. You choose what's real and what isn't as you meet some of the characters who actually lived during the Star Gate Program's operation. Just remember in the end, and under direct orders from the CIA… this never happened.

Fictional characters or factual characters...you decide who's who.

Sergeant Major Seth Phoenix: Army Special Forces and top remote viewer known for supernatural "gifts" in telekinesis.

General Douglas Monroe: Major General who witnesses Seth Phoenix's extraordinary abilities and reports the event to the CIA. He is the Deputy Commanding Officer of the U.S. Army Special Operations Command at Fort Bragg.

Dr. Nathaniel O'Connor: The Star Gate program's physician and researcher for the past decade.

Steven Pomerantz: Director of the Counterterrorism Division, FBI (Retired June 1995).

General Gordon R. Sullivan: Chief of Staff of the United States Army (Retired June 1995).

John Mark Deutch: Director of the CIA (May 1995-December 1996).

Nikita Oleshun: Russian psychic spy with telekinetic powers equal to Seth Phoenix.

"It is foolish and wrong to mourn the men who died. Rather, we should thank God that such men lived."

~ General George S. Patton

CHAPTER 1

Memorial Day, May 25, 1995
Fort Bragg, North Carolina
0500 hours

The sun had barely peaked above the horizon when its early rays covered one of the largest Army installations in the United States that housed more than 40,000 men and women. The mostly still, cool air now smelled of smoke and burning debris as an occasional breeze swept through the trees across thousands of acres. The Army base that covered over 250 square miles and served as home to the United States Army Airborne Forces and Special Forces was now a victim of terrorism. The stench of sulfur threatened to choke any survivors left buried beneath busted concrete and splintered wood. It happened in the soldiers' barracks where two Islamic extremists with links to Al Qaeda were living and working among American soldiers. Their plan had been in the making for months before they orchestrated a surprise attack and detonated a bomb, blasting the front section of the building apart and killing at least a dozen innocent people.

A raw, stinging sensation covered the soldier's bloody hands as he felt the weight of the steel beams and dry wall pressing against him, remnants from the massive explosion. A sickening silence lingered among the men trapped in the barracks. It seemed like hours, yet it was only minutes as military personnel and outside law enforcement agencies swarmed the area. Strong commands could be heard in the distance as officers moved in closer to the explosion site. The pulsating red and blue lights of emergency vehicles lit up the scene as survivors rushed away from an adjacent building now suspected to be wired to explode.

Sergeant Major Seth Phoenix groaned as he worked to move and stretch his arms free from the rubble. He glanced around the area where he had been standing just moments before. As his eyes scanned the area for any sign of life, he noticed movement in the far-right corner. Imminent danger took the form of a man, a terrorist who stood nearby, disguised by the American Army uniform that he wore.

It was life or death as the terrorist kept a dead aim right toward him. Seth froze and observed the terrorist's movements as the terrorist now stood over two soldiers who appeared to be lifeless. Seth assessed the situation from where he lay covered in dust and shards of glass. He saw what looked to be a dead body near the terrorist and realized that the suspected corpse was wearing body armor and may have been his accomplice.

Suddenly, he realized that the downed soldiers were still alive as he heard a low grunt and detected movement. Then just as they began to stir, he heard the terrorist shout orders to the injured men, jabbing one of them with the barrel of his rifle. He kicked the soldier in the face, causing him to fall over as the soldier attempted to stand.

A sudden rigor consumed the length of Seth's body. His heart thumped like that of a lion hunting prey, and though the heat from the explosion still lingered in the area, he could feel his body temperature begin to rise as he watched and waited.

Seth's body composition was changing. Within seconds, his energy placement would be unrestrained. As he breathed in deeply, he flinched as his vision shifted to a mental clarity unknown to most mankind. All of his senses were experiencing a sort of definition that swelled and morphed into something else, something so secret and so powerful that no one had ever been privy to this knowledge outside of his immediate family. He had been guarded his entire life. Exposure could cause him certain death or worse, it could ensure life as a lab rat. And his family couldn't take that chance.

Seth knew he had to act quickly and risk exposing his lifelong secret, but watching his friends die beneath the barrel of a terrorist's weapon was not an option. His heart rate sped up. Beads of sweat trailed over his body as he felt the familiar vibration from within. His metabolism was spiking quickly, his energy rising and spiraling out of control. He closed his eyes as he struggled to still himself. If he lost it, this power known only as his lifelong secret could cause more harm to the wounded soldiers. He slowly bent his legs closer together as he inched forward beneath the rubble. The terrorist heard movement and crouched low to the ground as he moved to investigate the area where Seth lay hidden.

Seth's breathing became rapid as the steel beams that lay scattered around him began to vibrate. The vibrations resembled a minor earthquake as Seth struggled to focus on the assailant while trying to get his footing in the rubble. He could tell that the terrorist was dazed and confused, his face twisted into a diabolical expression as he stepped over debris and tried to maintain his own footing. With a hard jerk, the terrorist swung around, his rifle suddenly pointing into the face of the two soldiers. He breathed fast and hard as he shouted at them and positioned his finger on the trigger, eager to shed more innocent blood.

Seth rose from the ground, his body literally lifting into midair as he let out a roar. He was covered in ash and dirt, and his piercing blue eyes seemed to glow as they penetrated everything around him. He raised his hands and pointed them toward a nearby steel beam lying directly in front of the terrorist. The terrorist stood rigid and stared at Seth in awe and disbelief, his eyes fixed on the sergeant major. He watched Seth levitate a steel beam right in front of him. His legs began to tremble as he lifted his rifle to shoot.

Seth positioned the beam in front of the terrorist and aimed it directly at the center of his chest. Just as the terrorist pulled back on the trigger, a powerful force propelled the steel beam toward him. The two soldiers quickly covered their heads as dust and dirt swirled around them. They heard the terrorist scream split seconds before the steel beam penetrated his chest. The impact knocked him backward, and he fell to the ground with the beam protruding from his back. Blood gushed from his body and formed a pool around him.

Seth rushed over to the soldiers who now lay dazed and disoriented. They stared at Seth, their mouths gaping open. They were speechless but eager to escape the area as Seth carried them to safety, one soldier on each arm, while they maneuvered through the remains of what had once been their sleeping quarters. As the three limped to safety, they coughed and gasped, struggling to breathe fresh air, their lungs full of smoke and soot from the explosion.

Seth made his way to a plush, grassy area and eased the soldiers off his arms, placing them flat against the ground. He stared in grave amazement at the scene unfolding before him. He wondered how this could have happened, how an unknown and seemingly undetected terrorist could be living among them, and all this time. And might there be more?

"Hey, Nick." Seth patted the shoulder of one of his closest friends in the unit, whom he'd brought from the rubble to safety.

"Hey, man." The two soldiers' eyes met. Nick rolled his head to the side.

"You're hurt. Help is coming." Seth's voice was strong but gritty, as his body had been regenerating from the sudden energy expulsion earlier.

"I got hit in the back. Something knocked me to the ground. I feel like my insides are crushed." Nick rubbed his hand across his stomach and grimaced in pain. A twelve-inch gash covered his abdominal section, and severe bruising was visible from the ripped and torn pants that barely covered his left leg.

Seth reached for the other soldier's hand. "Hey, Finley. You ok?"

Finley coughed and opened his eyes in a squint as he looked at Seth. "Hell, no, I am not ok. Do I look like I am ok? What the living hell just happened?"

Seth gave Finley a half-cocked grin. Finley McCall would be fine. His right kneecap was covered in abrasions after landing hard and fast on his knees when the roof caved in. It might be shattered, but he had managed to get out without any major injuries.

Finley's eyes stayed fixed on Seth as he studied his friend. Seth noticed his inquisitive stare. He knew Finley had witnessed a supernatural phenomenon that he wouldn't be able to explain to anyone. Seth had been born with these abilities, abilities that he had wrestled with all of his life. It was the reason he had few close friends. He simply lived his life trapped in a world that very few people understood. It was his own prison, but one he was forced to endure.

Emergency personnel spotted the men and rushed to the area where Finley and Nick lay. Seth motioned for the paramedics to check Nick first. He stood by Finley's side as they both watched them prepare to move Nick.

Finley turned to Seth and searched his face. "Sergeant Major, you saved my life back there. You saved all of us."

Seth nodded once. "Yes." He knew Finley wanted to ask him questions.

"Phoenix?"

Seth stood silent and looked away.

"How did you force a ten-foot, 400 lb. steel beam to rise in mid-air and then shoot it into that guy's chest?"

Seth studied the ground, not wanting to answer. "You saw that?"

Finley nodded. "What the fuck was that?"

Seth jerked around and quickly placed his index finger over his lips. He whispered through gritted teeth. "We'll talk later. Just shut up. Don't tell any fucking body what you saw. Do you understand?"

"Are you kidding me? You think this shit won't leak? Other people saw it, man. But I owe you my life. You saved us." Finley's whispers were still loud.

Seth leaned over Finley while the paramedics worked to get Nick onto a stretcher.

"Look, I don't wanna be a damn hero. What you just saw needs to be treated as highly classified 'don't tell a fucking soul' Intel. I need you to keep this on the down low. I mean it. If this leaks, my life is fucked."

Finley stared at Seth in disbelief. "Shit, man. You're fucked then because Monroe watched us as we came out. He was standing right there. He saw everything."

Seth's skin became cold. His stomach churned. Fear crept in, and he began to feel faint. He kneeled down to rest on his ankles. The paramedics wheeled Finley to the back of the ambulance as Seth quickly gained composure, his breathing deep but controlled. He stood and rubbed his hands through the soft, dark stubble of his military-style haircut. He contemplated what had just occurred and whether Monroe might have really seen everything. If so, the general had witnessed first-hand evidence of the supernatural ability that Seth had fought his whole life to keep hidden. As he began to walk away from the flashing emergency lights and the remnants of the explosion, he turned to face the general walking straight toward him. The general stopped and stared at Seth as if issuing an order. His stance and facial expression commanded submission as Seth slowly approached.

"Sergeant Major Phoenix." Monroe waited. His thoughts were well hidden as he watched the young, thirty-four-year-old sergeant major walking toward him. His face was without expression, but Seth knew what the general had to do. If Monroe had seen what he thought he had seen, then the CIA and the White House would have to be notified immediately. He had only heard of these abilities in a controlled environment, but the military project he knew of had not produced such performance in its two decades of operation.

"General Monroe, Sir." Seth stopped and stood off to the side of the general. He maintained a quiet disposition.

"Are you okay, Sergeant Major?"

"Yes, Sir. I am okay."

Monroe nodded. "I need you to report to my office tomorrow at 0700 hours."

Phoenix hesitated before speaking as a sense of doom overshadowed him. There was no point in asking the general "why". Seth answered, "Yes, Sir."

Just as the general turned, he stopped and motioned for Seth to wait. "You tell no one about our meeting tomorrow morning. Do you understand? From this point on, Sergeant Major, any repertoire that you and I have is to be treated as highly classified." The general stared at Seth with fierce eyes as he gave these final orders.

"Yes, Sir." Seth nodded. As the general walked away, Seth watched him disappear until he became nothing more than a shadow. A sense of dread consumed him as his mind reeled with visions and premonitions of what awaited him within the next 48 hours. His lifelong secret had now been revealed before a U.S. Army general, and the consequences were going to be massive.

CHAPTER 2

The General's office.
Tuesday, 0700 hours

General Monroe's voice was low and gruff as he spoke into the phone receiver. "How will I know who he is?"

The voice at the other end of the phone answered with authority, his words curt and fast, leaving no time to be repeated.

"He'll be driving an unmarked vehicle, a silver Tahoe, and he'll be dressed in civilian clothes. You may inform Sergeant Major Phoenix that he is being moved immediately. The driver will be there within an hour. Anything else?"

"No."

"General, if he is who you say he is, then this could spark a global manhunt. You and I have never spoken."

"Affirmative."

The phone went silent. Monroe sat down in the faded leather chair behind his desk and adjusted the lapel on his jacket. His coat carried the ribbons of a man who had served in five wars with three Silver Stars and two Legion of Merit awards under his belt. He was an Army Ranger and Green Beret who once commanded the First Infantry Division, known as the "Big Red One". Now the 48-year-old general was the Deputy Commanding Officer of the United States Army Special Operations Command at Fort Bragg.

He scratched his brow and sighed. He glanced around the room; his thoughts consumed with the reality of carrying this new knowledge. He knew Seth Phoenix was being transported to Fort Meade. He knew there were secret projects being conducted within the Army, but his knowledge of the Star Gate program had been somewhat limited until now because the CIA had the Army general on a "need to know basis". How Seth Phoenix was about to be used by the United States Army was only speculation in the general's mind, but he knew that Seth Phoenix's life as he knew it was now officially over.

Meanwhile, Seth Phoenix packed the last remaining items of clothing that he had managed to salvage from the total destruction of his barracks the day before. His mind raced as he sat down on one of the cots that had been provided to the soldiers left homeless from the blast. The unit had been relocated to temporary housing near the West side of the base. He sighed as he checked his watch. It was time to move out. He picked up his bag and headed for the general's office.

His facial expression was void, and his eyes moistened as he thought of home. His mother and father had fought to protect him all of his life. Maybe he should have just stayed in Tennessee. Maybe he had made a foolish mistake by joining the military, thinking that he could actually escape from a secret that he struggled to keep hidden every day of his life. Except for his parents, no one knew, nor could they likely have understood, that he had been born a star child, a child believed to possess innate gifts such as telepathic communication, knowledge of human energy fields, and extraordinary psychic abilities. His eyes were the typical sky blue that was most often seen in and associated with star children, a blue so intense that they appeared almost translucent during periods of extreme energy dissipation. And during periods of heightened psychic awareness or metabolic changes, Seth became famished, his appetite insatiable as his body required a high-calorie intake to sustain him.

Seth used both sides of his brain. Evidence of this was first revealed when he was a young boy. It was his turn to bat that day on the baseball field, but he struggled to find a comfortable position as he fidgeted at the home plate. The coach noticed the familiar behavior that he had seen before in a five-year-old. They were ambidextrous. Blessed with the ability to efficiently use both arms, it was an aggravation at times. The coach assisted Seth and instructed him to pick a side. Seth looked at the coach, who nodded at him. He hesitated for a moment before positioning himself as a left-handed batter. That day would set the course for the remainder of his school days, as he would eventually become a left-handed writer also.

As Seth walked the ten-minute trek to the general's office, his mind raced with visions. His senses were heightened. Even his sense of smell resembled that of ancient ancestors who had relied on pure instinct for survival. He heard a large vehicle approaching but saw nothing. He knew he was having premonitions at that moment. He was sensing the very things he would experience within the hour. His departure from the base would be quick and secret as he would be escorted away. He heard talking and realized that he was hearing a conversation that had already taken place. It was the general. And he had already reported the incident with Seth Phoenix.

More images flooded Seth's mind, like a silent movie reel spinning in his head. He stopped for a moment on the sidewalk as he neared the door to the general's office. He breathed deep and surveyed the area around him.

Someone was coming for him. He was being transported to another unit, another base far away. He couldn't see anything at the moment, but he knew he was heading to a secluded, restricted area used primarily for government research. Suddenly, the door to the general's office flung open. Standing in front of his desk in the small, crowded room, the general held the door open and stared at Seth as he motioned for him to come inside.

Seth kept quiet as he hurried in. Monroe motioned for him to sit down as he casually leaned against the desk in front of him. He didn't want Seth to become intimidated. He didn't need any trouble. Even though he had soldiers who stood close by and ready to help if he needed them, he didn't want to draw any attention to their meeting. This had to be done without anyone questioning the sergeant major's departure.

The general leaned close to Seth and lowered his voice even though no one else was in the room with them. "Sergeant Major, you know why you are here."

Seth's stiff composure didn't waver as his eyes rolled upward to meet the general's stare.

"Yes, Sir. I know."

Monroe nodded. "Sergeant Major, in just a few minutes, you will be transported to a highly restricted area very few people know about. There will be multiple escorts accompanying you along the way. I have no more information except to tell you that it is near Fort Meade."

Seth's eyes stayed fixed on the general. "Yes, Sir. I already know."

"What do you mean, you already know?" The general squinted as he studied Seth's face.

"Sir, I have senses that other people wouldn't understand. I know things I probably shouldn't know about, like the conversation that you just had on the phone before I got here." Seth leaned back to put distance between them.

Monroe's face was tense as he watched Seth and listened. He wanted to hear more. He rotated his hand in the air, motioning for Seth to continue.

"You're transferring me to a lab where I will basically be a guinea pig for a bunch of researchers who don't know what the hell they should be looking for in the first place. My life is fucked now. Thank you very much."

"Sergeant Major, you could be one of the most significant advancements in the history of our weapons technology and the way we gather Intel if you are who we think you are. You have an opportunity to change the world. Literally."

Seth remained silent. He wanted isolation, and he wanted it now. "Who do you think I am, General?" Seth's hands began to tingle as he became more and more anxious. He rubbed his hands together and sat rigidly in the chair.

The general looked at Seth and hesitated for a moment. "Sergeant Major, have you ever heard of a military project called Star Gate?"

Seth could read the general's thoughts. Words and images swished in and out of his mind like an ocean tide. He picked up various sentences and quickly pieced them together. He had never heard of Star Gate, but within seconds of receiving telepathic information, he was now informed of the military's top psychic spy program. However, Seth decided to play dumb.

"No, I have not."

The general maintained an emotionless stance, careful not to show any reaction to the sergeant major's answers, but he felt his eyes squint as he studied Seth. He doubted anything that he said. He figured Phoenix might have heard about Star Gate through a leak. Surely someone with his extraordinary abilities already knew about the program that had been in operation since the late 1970's. He nodded and looked at the door as if he was making sure that no one was about to enter the room.

"Star Gate has been in operation since 1978. It is a secret project facilitated by the Army for the purpose of training psychic spies."

Seth looked at the general with raised eyebrows.

"You think I am psychic, General? All humans possess psychic abilities."

"We think you may be extraordinary, and we need to find out more. You will receive more information within the next few hours, but for now, you need to trust what we are telling you."

"This blast last night. This was Al Qaeda, wasn't it?" Seth probed the general.

"Yes, we now believe that Fort Bragg was only the first target. There are people all over now. Don't expect much sleep for the next few days."

Seth nodded. He now knew what his mission would involve, but how far would the military push him? And how much of his powers would they demand to see?

Seth heard the sound of tires on loose gravel almost one mile away. "Your driver is coming."

General Monroe nodded once.

Seth stood and saluted the general. He walked to the office door and waited. Monroe motioned for him to stay quiet and hidden from view as he glanced outside. The SUV pulled around and slowly came to a stop directly in front of the building. A man in civilian clothes exited the vehicle and quickly walked around to the passenger side. Monroe grabbed the office door handle and signaled for Seth to head out.

The unknown driver opened the front passenger door. Seth jumped in as the driver raced to the other side.

The driver got into the vehicle and turned to study Seth. "What is your name?"

Seth looked puzzled but answered. "Sergeant Major Seth Phoenix, Sir."

"Do you know who I am?" The man was curt.

"No, Sir. No, I don't."

"And you will not. My job is to inform you of where you will be going and of what you can expect. You will change vehicles again before reaching your final destination. You are not to ask questions at this point. Just listen and follow directions as if your life depends on it because it does, Sergeant Major." He slammed the gearshift into drive and pressed the accelerator, driving fast toward the main exit off the base.

"Yes, Sir." Seth kept his eyes fixed straight ahead. He didn't flinch. He literally felt his body stiffen, as if it were part of the seat. His mental awareness began to peak as his mind bounced back and forth, remembering his home and his two friends, Nick and Finley. Suddenly, he realized that they may be sequestered by the military because of their association with him.

"You are being transferred to Fort Meade, where you will be assigned to a restricted area. I have no knowledge of where you will be staying, except that it is within the base. You are being transferred to the most classified and restricted area of our military's Intel research. I am not privy to the nature of the research. Anyone who knows what goes on within those walls carries with them a secret that could cost them their life. You are being transferred on a top-secret mission because it is believed that you can help our government locate and destroy hidden Al Qaeda cells in this country and worldwide. You are not to discuss any details with family members or with others outside your unit. To do so could put you and your family in immediate danger. Do you understand?" The driver sounded robotic as he spoke.

Seth was barely able to mumble. "Yes, Sir."

"After you arrive at the unit, the Army will begin a series of tests to determine the strength of your abilities. Please do not be alarmed. You are in the safest place you could possibly be on the planet. If the tests determine that you indeed have supernatural capabilities, we will position an undercover post to stand watch over and protect your family members. However, they are not to be informed of our presence. Your cooperation is imperative, Sergeant Major. This is a case of national security."

Seth nodded and gave the driver a 'thumbs up' as he verbally accepted his responsibility to the United States of America. "Yes, Sir. I understand."

In less than 24 hours, Seth Phoenix would become the most top-secret government weapon in the entire world.

CHAPTER 3

Hours later, they arrived at an abandoned Army airfield in southeast North Carolina. The area was once a Confederate Civil War fort along the Atlantic coast, but it now remained desolate and forgotten, except for the Army's occasional classified use. Today, the landing strip heavily used during World War II would serve as the site where Seth Phoenix would board a Beechcraft C-12 Huron, a military transport aircraft now headed to Fort Meade, Maryland.

The driver pulled the SUV onto the abandoned runway, where vegetation had begun to grow, forming a spiderweb of grassy trails as it busted through the concrete. He parked near the plane where a team of three people dressed in Army fatigues waited for Seth's arrival. The driver motioned for Seth to get out of the vehicle and follow him.

As the driver escorted Seth toward the plane, the three men turned and began to board the aircraft. The pilot and co-pilot took their seats upon entering the cockpit and immediately prepared for flight, fastening their seatbelts and adjusting their headgear. The third crew member waited at the steps to the side entrance. Seth climbed the steps and followed the soldier into the plane, but just before the soldier reached to close the door, Seth turned to look back at the SUV driver, only to find that both he and the vehicle had suddenly high-tailed it out of the area.

The aircraft engines cranked up, preparing for takeoff. The humming and thumping sound of the blades created a high, shrill noise that still penetrated the headgear Seth had been given to wear. He sat back and pulled the seat belt tight, adjusting the fit. He glanced at the crew chief who had been observing him. The three men manning the aircraft had been given very little information about whom they would be transporting, but they had been instructed to take precautions with the passenger and to be alert to any anxiety he displayed before or during the flight. Top personnel at Star Gate knew what havoc Seth Phoenix could cause to an aircraft's navigation system if his molecular structure suddenly dispersed an explosion of uncontrolled energy.

"Sergeant Major, you ok?" The crew chief shouted above the thunder of the engines. He reached into his pocket and handed Seth a Xanax pill, used to treat anxiety and induce relaxation. The crew had been given strict instructions to ensure that Sergeant Major Phoenix swallowed the pill for everyone's safety on board.

Seth nodded and gave the chief a thumbs-up, but he hesitated in taking the medicine. He looked at the soldier.

"Why this?" Seth knew what it was. His senses had picked up on the feelings of the crew when he entered the plane.

"I was told to give you this for relaxation. You will be meeting Dr. O'Connor in a little while. He doesn't want to take any chances with you." The soldier nodded toward the pill in Seth's hand, motioning for him to go ahead and take the meds.

Seth picked up the bottled water beside him and tossed the pill to the back of his throat. He took a long drink as the soldier watched him satisfy their request. As the plane lifted off the ground, Phoenix leaned back and closed his eyes, taking a two-hour nap in the sky.

Somewhere near Fort Meade, Maryland
May 27, 1995
Dusk

Seth awoke to find himself exiting the plane and getting into another unmarked vehicle that would transport him to the final destination. He climbed into the passenger side front seat and fastened his seatbelt for another thirty-minute ride, otherwise known as the path to "nowhere land".

Phoenix wasn't familiar with any of the area's geography, but he paid close attention to the winding roads leading into a secluded, wooded area. Because it was now dusk, it was hard to detect his surroundings. His heightened instincts would have to be called upon, but for now, he would save his energy and simply observe everything happening around him.

The driver stopped the vehicle on a dead-end trail surrounded by trees and overgrowth. Suddenly, two men dressed in normal Army fatigues appeared from what must have been an underground tunnel. Seth watched as one of them approached the passenger side of the vehicle and opened the door.

"Sergeant Major Phoenix, welcome to Fort Meade. Put this hood over your head before exiting the vehicle. There's a vent for your mouth, and you'll see the clear window for your eyes, but your peripheral vision will be blocked." Dr. Nathaniel

O'Connor pushed the headgear into Seth's hands and waited for him to position the hood. He stood directly in front of Seth and waited for him to step out of the vehicle.

Seth stepped out of the passenger side door, one foot at a time, and stretched his legs for a brief moment. His 6'3" statue towered over the doctor's 5'9" frame. He studied the doctor and immediately formed an impression of him. He would be an ally. He was the chief doctor on a team of seven. The unit also included personnel such as office administrators and custodians. As Seth reached out to shake the doctor's hand, a surge of information was transferred to his mind. His body jerked. He quickly regained composure, not wanting to alarm the doctor or others, but at that moment, he sensed the doctor's emotional and psychological state. Images of the doctor's family life and childhood flashed in and out of his mind's eye. He realized that the doctor had strong, almost exceptional bonds with his two grown children and his wife, whom he affectionately called "Blondie".

Seth fastened the hood in place as the doctor led him down a dark corridor toward a staircase directly in front of him. He was being led underground. Seth could not see anything other than what was directly in front of him, but he managed to determine that the area where he was going to be spending most of his time was a secret bunker deep within a wooded area near Fort Meade.

Dr. O'Connor opened a bomb proof door after placing his thumb over the fingerprint scanner. He and Seth walked to the second door, which had a retina scanner and keypad. The doctor placed his eye socket firmly against the pad and stared forward into a blue light that flashed once upon recognition. He then typed in a secret code as assigned exclusively to his identity and waited for the system to acknowledge and approve his entry. A loud, commanding buzz sounded as the door lock opened and the two men entered the hidden compound, fully equipped with living quarters, a mini-medical facility about the size of a small physician's office, and several rooms with an examination table and a large, cushioned reclining chair. The underground compound seemed limitless, its hallways winding through a vast network of tunnels.

Dr. O'Connor opened a side door and led Seth into a conference room. It looked like any other conference room with a table, bottled water stacked in a nearby corner, and twenty-four rolling padded chairs.

"You can have a seat, Sergeant Major. Go ahead and remove the hood." Dr. O'Connor sat across from Seth. Two other Army officers entered the room and sat down next to the doctor. "Have you slept at all during your trip here?"

Seth nodded. "Yes, sir. A little."

"Do you know why you have been transported here?"

"Yes, I was told by the driver who picked me up at Fort Bragg."

The doctor nodded once. The other officers sat quietly as if they were guarding the room against an unseen invasion. "Good. The first thing we will do is get you into your new quarters. You need to be rested and refreshed by 0800 hours. You'll have everything that you need, and you'll be comfortable. This will be an unusual environment for you, but nonetheless, you will be serving the United States of America in a different capacity if the testing proves positive. These guys will show you to your room. Do you have any questions? If so, make them brief."

Seth had tons of questions, but he already knew the answers to most of them. More than anything else, he needed sleep and recuperation. He shook his head. "No, sir."

"See you in a few hours." The doctor got up and walked out the door as the two officers now led Seth Phoenix down another long hallway leading to one of several rooms with a queen-sized bed and a shower that Seth could call his own. It actually resembled a small hotel room equipped with satellite television, a phone, and a minibar. The rooms had been designed and built for personnel such as scientists and doctors working in the Star Gate program who required overnight accommodation. He had not had this kind of comfort in months. It was a welcome break, at least for the moment.

Seth tossed his bag to the corner of the bed. He removed his shirt and pulled the covers back as he slid into the softness of cool, cotton sheets and plump goose feather pillows stacked neatly at the head of the bed. A long sigh escaped from his lips as he drifted fast asleep.

As the morning sun began to peak over the woods that shielded the underground entrance like a canopy, Seth's body began to move out of deep sleep. He rolled from side to side, not wanting to awaken completely. He drifted in and out of consciousness until suddenly he felt trapped in a dream where someone's icy cold fingers were wrapped around his throat. His vision was blocked, and he struggled to force his eyelids open. He felt his hands and feet bound together by ropes that had rubbed his skin raw. His wrists now burned and bled, and he could hear cries overhead. An unseen force had managed to overpower him during his most vulnerable state of sleep rejuvenation, when his powers were weakened. His mind raced as he formed conclusions. Someone must have known about his weakness, but failing to recognize his strength would be their ultimate mistake.

Seth lay very still as he felt the blade of a knife pushing against his cheek. He smelled the breath of what he sensed was a male figure standing in front of him as he assessed his assailant. Suddenly, chatter filled the room. It was Arabic, and Seth was fast to interpret the conversation. He heard fragments of a conversation between two people discussing a terrorist plot. Seth attempted to calm himself, mentally focusing on his breathing. He did not want his body to start molecular transformation. He needed to get free, but he had to do it strategically because he had not yet determined where he was or how many of his captors were present.

A chair squeaked as the unknown assailant stood up and walked away. A faint light seeped through the room as the assailant opened the door and whispered to his accomplice. Unbeknownst to them, Seth Phoenix could hear and interpret every word with his heightened sense of hearing. A cold rush of doom washed over him. He knew he had to escape and stop the attack that was being planned right now as the terrorists set up operations at a major airport in the United States.

Seth closed his eyes tightly as he focused on the ropes binding his hands and feet. Sweat began to drip from his forehead as the ropes became singed and fell to the floor. The walls vibrated and shook as Seth stood and pointed toward the door where the two terrorists now stood staring at him in disbelief. With a sudden push, Seth propelled a burst of telekinetic energy forward. The door slammed shut against one of the man's hands and crushed his fingers between the jam. He screamed in pain, cursing as Seth pushed his palm out in front of him, projecting the telekinetic force hard and fast. But just before it could annihilate the enemy, one of the men snapped the AK-47 rifle fast in the air and pulled the trigger.

The officer knocked, then pushed the door open and flicked on the light. "Sergeant Major, it's 0600. Plans have changed. We need you downstairs in forty-five minutes. Get moving."

Seth Phoenix stirred. Where the hell was he, and what the hell had just happened to him? He was safe in the same bed he had gotten into a few hours earlier. But just minutes ago, he was fighting for his life after having been bound and gagged. He sat up and let his eyes wander around the room. Then a sudden knowing came to him. He had been dreaming, but he hoped it was simply a nightmare and not a premonition of darker things to come. It had been months since he had a precognitive dream. He jumped out of the bed and headed for the shower. He turned the water faucet on and waited for the water to warm as he wiped his eyes and took a deep breath. If this dream was precognitive, all hell was about to break loose.

CHAPTER 4

Dr. O'Connor hurried down the long corridor toward another secret meeting room, where three specially trained intelligence officers sat waiting, along with two other unnamed top-secret officials. That's the way the program was run. Only a handful of people knew anything about the government's psychic research. And those who knew were required to sign an oath stating that they "knew nothing" about the program if ever questioned. Confidentiality wasn't negotiable.

Dr. O'Connor reached for the doorknob and pushed it open. Two uniform officers greeted the doctor at the door as he entered the meeting room.

"Good morning, gentlemen." The doctor looked surprised as he noticed General Monroe standing across from the entrance.

"General Monroe." The doctor's tone was inquisitive.

Monroe reached and offered the doctor a handshake as he nodded "hello".

"Gentlemen." The doctor pointed to the chairs surrounding the table, inviting the others to sit with him.

Monroe cleared his voice and leaned forward. "Dr. O'Connor, I was brought here to pass along what I witnessed at the base. Sergeant Major Phoenix was incapacitated after the explosion along with two other soldiers in the west wing barracks. The men were buried beneath a lot of debris and some 400 lb. steel ceiling beams. It was a wonder that they survived."

The doctor listened with intent. He nodded and blinked in response to the general's comments, giving him a sign that he was fully aware of the situation.

"As I made my way to the west wing, I thought I heard talking. The front section of the building was completely blown away, but there were sections of walls that withstood the blast."

The doctor lifted his hand and motioned for the general to pause. "The two soldiers who were with Seth Phoenix. Where are they now?"

"They are still at Fort Bragg in temporary housing."

The doctor breathed in deep. "And they also witnessed Seth Phoenix lift 400 lb. steel beams?"

The general nodded once. "Yes, that is correct."

The doctor glanced around the room. He shook his head. "Has anyone questioned these men? Why the hell are they in temporary housing?"

"They aren't being held, Doctor. But they have been questioned, and the proper protocol was used when discussing this situation."

"Proper protocol?"

"Yes, they were required to sign the oath."

Dr. O'Connor pushed his chair back and started to stand. He turned and addressed the uniformed officers at the door. "Where is Seth Phoenix now?"

"In his room, Sir."

The doctor pointed at the door. "Get him in here."

Thirty minutes later and fifteen minutes early, Seth walked out of the room and was escorted to the same familiar conference area. As he entered the room, he was met with faces he had not seen the night before. The room was filled with low murmurs and whispers, ongoing at the same time. Seth walked over to a nearby chair and waited as every eye in the room suddenly became fixed on him. Dr. O'Connor made his way to Seth's side.

"Gentlemen, meet Sergeant Major Seth Phoenix."

Seth nodded as a flood of devastating news swished into his inner realms. At that moment, he knew what the doctor was about to announce. The room was dead silent.

The doctor's pupils were dilated, and the lines in his forehead tightened as he leaned closer to Seth before he addressed the group. In a low, compelling, and grave tone, the doctor urged Seth.

"Sergeant Major, we have to work fast. We just received intel from an informant that puts an attack in exactly 72 hours."

Seth felt the blood leave his face as his body suddenly got a chill upon hearing what he considered a confirmation of his earlier dream. He was almost stoic as he sat and listened to the doctor. He glanced around the room at the other men and noticed General Monroe's eyes fixed on him.

"I need you to tell us who you are and how you got these abilities? Have you had these powers your entire life? And what else can you do?" The doctor gave Seth a compassionate but equally inquisitive look and spoke in a non-threatening, friendly tone. He had to have Seth Phoenix's total cooperation, or the operation would be over before they could even appoint him to the role they had planned for him.

"You already know who I am." Seth wanted confirmation of the investigation currently being performed on him, but he knew no one in the room would volunteer the information. Whatever he wanted to know, he would have to get it by supernatural means, in a way that no one knew what he was doing. He could become an enemy to them just as quickly as he was an ally if he didn't exercise extreme caution.

The doctor nodded. "And your parents, your friends. Even your dog. But that doesn't tell us everything we need to know. Who are you?"

"I have never told anybody. My entire life has been guarded and lived in secrecy. Do you understand? Do you understand the consequences of exposing this now?" Seth Phoenix clenched his fist and leaned forward toward the doctor and the general who now sat across from them.

Seth spoke with a firm certainty. "I must have protection now."

"As we promised you." The doctor looked at the general, who acknowledged the comment and nodded in agreement.

Seth hesitated and then took a deep breath before disclosing his true identity. "I was born a star child. I have heightened senses beyond normal human capacity. My instinctual urges surpass those of an animal. I hear by clairaudience. My vision is normal, but my ability to see things at a distance is due to clairvoyance. I'm able to communicate telepathically, but most people don't know how. However, I am not omniscient. I do not know everything, and my abilities are not completely foolproof. My margin of error is approximately three percent. Sometimes I see things that are manifestations of emotion rather than precognitive events, but these visions have to be treated with the same discrimination. While it is true that I can astral travel, I cannot be everywhere at once. In other words, I am not God. And my abilities are not easily manipulated, but I can summon the power of psychokinesis in extreme situations."

The doctor studied Seth. "And certainly, this attack on Fort Bragg warranted the use of your abilities, Sergeant Major Phoenix."

Seth rubbed the side of his face and turned his head in a half-cocked position as he nodded once. "Yes, it did, Sir."

"Sergeant Major, can you explain to the rest of us what a star child is?" General Monroe was ready to ask his own questions. He twirled a pen between his fingers and abruptly stopped as Seth began to speak.

"A star child is a child born with supernatural capabilities. It is complex, but I know what you want. You have spent almost two decades searching for the ultimate psychic spy."

"Then you know about this program, Star Gate?"

"No."

The room was silent. An expression of simultaneous curiosity and confusion covered some of the men's faces.

"I know about Star Gate now. I had no reason to know about the program until the general ordered me to his office. It was at that point that I was able to see and ultimately learn about its past history."

"How?" The general's eyes were fixed on Seth.

Seth hesitated. "I-I don't know how to explain it, Sir."

Dr. O'Connor interjected. "Sergeant Major, I'm going to do an MRI. There is a portion of your brain that I need to see. I am looking for something specific that will confirm your capabilities and everything you are telling us. Think of it as a form of brain tattoo. We have seen this in other special agents. It is a unique calling card that thirty percent of the population has, but most of them aren't aware of it. If you have these distinct features, you are possibly using more than 20% of your brain's capacity. That alone would make you superhuman and unlike any other human being in the history of our evolution." The doctor motioned for the men to exit the room.

"Your two friends also witnessed your ability, is that correct?" asked General Monroe. He was stalling the men from leaving to find out whether Finley or Nick had tried to contact Seth.

"Yes, sir." Seth's concern was evident in his tone. He looked at the general and searched the general's face.

The general noticed Seth's anxiety. "They are not being held, but they were questioned. They have signed an oath declaring that they will not ever discuss this occurrence with anyone else."

Seth felt some relief, but he realized the danger that he had exposed them to. This type of news never remained classified. And anyone who believed that the government or military could guarantee this would remain top secret was fooling themselves. Somehow, somewhere, it would leak, and Seth knew it. "And my parents? Are they safe?"

"We have security posted close to your parents' home. We are watching. If we need to, we are prepared to move them."

The Intel unit had already moved quickly to provide safety and security to Seth's family. In order for the CIA to have Seth's full cooperation, they had to have complete confidence in them and their willingness to protect him and his family from any outside threats. The Star Gate operation depended on it. And the lives of millions of Americans depended on Seth Phoenix's supernatural ability to sense what was about to happen. He was coming into his destiny. He was, without question, the United States Military's most lethal weapon now.

Dr. O'Connor moved to the door. "We have to get the sergeant major into the lab now. If our Intel is correct, we have only three days to stop another attack."

Seth Phoenix stood boldly facing the men. He spoke in a loud, clear tone, with urgency and determination, to be taken seriously.

"You said 72 hours. We no longer have 72 hours, Sir. The next attack is *tomorrow*."

CHAPTER 5

Seth lay completely still inside the windowless, almost soundproof remote-viewing lab. The temperature remained cool at 70 degrees Fahrenheit, with only a soft, glowing lamp on a nearby table. He drifted into the recesses of another dimension where he viewed events happening before him in what seemed like real time.

Seth shuddered uncontrollably as he watched hundreds of FBI agents and undercover law enforcement officers surrounding the world's busiest airport, waiting for a team of suspected terrorists under the command of Al Qaeda leader Emir Hussain to enter the front ticketing area. This is what Seth Phoenix had seen in a vision earlier that day, a vicious plot being orchestrated at the very moment he was seated in the conference room. A terrorist attack on the world's busiest airport would be an unprecedented victory in Al Qaeda's agenda for a high casualty count and to cause massive chaos by paralyzing travel around the world. Subsequently, it would allow them to attack multiple targets within the United States and abroad. Since acquiring American sympathizers and other followers already within the country, the terrorist organization had grown from a small membership of a few dozen men to an overwhelming count that now included more than three thousand.

As Seth Phoenix watched from his seat in the underground lab, he felt the men's movement around the perimeter of the airport. He positioned himself near the main entrance to the terminal. He watched as a dark-haired man parked his car and exited the vehicle, walking fast toward the main terminal entrance.

Seth heard chatter. It sounded like radio chatter as FBI members gave instructions to the team. Seth suddenly realized that the military had already positioned and informed a kill team to shoot on sight. A suspected suicide bomber would have to be stopped before he could detonate the bomb. As horrific as it seemed, this was now a war in a civilian territory. It had come to this: a fight to protect our people and our way of life within our own boundaries. And the rules had to change when faced with the possibility of mass extinction due to acts of terrorism.

Seth mumbled aloud. "He's wearing a gray sports jacket, like a Members Only jacket. He's walking toward the entrance. He has blue sneakers with a white stripe and tan pants. Looks like cargo pants. He has black hair. About 5'10" tall and 175 pounds. He walks funny. He's pigeon-toed. Wait. He has a scar on the side of his left cheek. I am inside his energy field. I need to get the hell out of here. Wait. He is pledging loyalty to Emir Hussain and the cause. I can hear him. He has volunteered to do..."

"Can you see that he has a bomb?" Dr. O'Connor interrupted and questioned Seth with urgency as he sat beside him, tracking his vital signs and recording every single word that Phoenix mumbled.

Seth began shouting, his body trembling. "It's taped to the inside of his chest and back. Holy Fuck! There are enough explosives there to level the whole fucking airport! Get out! Everybody get out!"

Seth's heart rate accelerated as medical equipment in the room began to blink and beep in unison. His temperature climbed dramatically. His fists were clenched, turning bright red, as Dr. O'Connor spoke calmly, instructing him to return from his meditative state. The doctor started counting down from three.

"Three, two, and one. Seth, you are here."

Seth jerked upright. The doctor's stethoscope flew violently across the room. The table Seth had been lying on suddenly slammed against the opposite wall. Seth quickly landed on his feet but then stumbled backward and fell against the opposite wall from where the table now rolled to the center of the room.

"Seth, you must get control!" Dr. O'Connor shouted.

Seth struggled to regain composure. His breathing slowly returned to normal as his eyes darted around the room.

"Sergeant Major, can you tell me if he is acting alone?" The doctor reached for Seth's arm and assisted him as he sat down.

Seth was silent for a moment. "It's a suicide bomber. He's alone, but he's carrying enough explosives to wipe out a huge portion of the airport. We have to stop them."

Dr. O'Connor rushed to the door. "Wait here!" he called back to Seth.

He ran down the hall and toward the testing lab. He flung the door to the testing lab open, where General Monroe and two of Star Gate's top officials were awaiting the doctor's report from Seth Phoenix's remote viewing session. All eyes were fixed on the doctor as he breathed hard and fast, his speech clipped and his tone commanding.

"Get the CIA on the phone."

"What the hell happened?" General Monroe stood up from his seat.

"Phoenix just had a precognitive experience. He saw what our Intel has been telling us for the past two weeks. He saw it and repeated it verbatim, as we know. We need to order a commando to that damn airport right now. Not tomorrow, not in a few hours, but right fucking now!"

"Wait a minute. How the hell do we trust this?" General Monroe wanted to be sure that they weren't jumping the gun in dispatching the commando, when perhaps what Seth might actually be seeing was intended to be a diversion of sorts, as an even larger attack was potentially underway somewhere else.

"General, with all due respect, you can have doubt and question the authenticity of remote viewing at a later date if you wish. And I can give you Seth Phoenix's whole damn file, but right now, we have no choice but to trust what he's telling us. We need to move on with this. And move now."

"Okay, okay." General Monroe lifted his hand in the air, giving him a "stop" signal. He sat down, shaking his head. "And I would like to know, what all those damn brain tests reveal about this man's supernatural ability? We still know very little about him."

"I can't believe you are questioning this, and especially now after you witnessed what he did at Fort Bragg. You reported it yourself, General." Dr. O'Connor was perplexed and suspicious.

"I know. I guess I'm just having a hard time accepting that we now have Superman on site, who can suddenly supply us with better Intel than all our other resources. We're the United States government, for fuck's sake. And he's just a boy. Could be a fucking sociopath, for all we know."

The room was dead silent as everyone waited for the doctor's explanation. They all had doubts. But no one dared to leave the room or take their eyes off the doctor until he settled the inquiry. Star Gate had comprised some of the most skilled remote viewers in the world, but no one had ever come as close in visual accuracy as Seth Phoenix. No one. Why was he so much more special than all the other remote viewers that the military had trained and put into service before him?

For the first time since he burst into the lab, Dr. O'Connor relaxed his shoulders and placed his hands in his pockets. He looked around the room at the multiple pairs of eyes staring at him insistently, demanding answers as he prepared to educate them on the differences between Seth Phoenix's brain and an average brain or even another remote viewer's brain. His tone was confident and calm as he spoke. He sighed inwardly to himself. This couldn't take long. Too much was at stake. Too many lives. And he needed their confidence.

"Gentlemen, earlier this morning, we discovered a vital key to Seth Phoenix's unique abilities. The brain scan revealed that a portion of Seth's brain is twice the size of a normal human brain."

"What are you talking about? What portion exactly?" General Monroe interrupted, his brows were furrowed, and his lips were tight in a frown.

"General, hear me out. There is a portion of the brain that tends to be enlarged in people with keen psychic abilities. I said 'enlarged'. But Seth Phoenix's corpus callosum is twice the size of even our most gifted remote viewers. It's unlike anything I have ever seen."

The general glanced around the room at the others before returning his eyes to the doctor. He listened, though now more intently, as the doctor resumed his explanation.

"The corpus callosum is a bundle of fibers that connects the two cerebral hemispheres. Seth is ambidextrous. He uses thirty to forty percent of his brain's capacity, whereas the average human is only using about ten percent. When he is in a meditative state, his energy seems to remain steady. But just a few minutes ago, this soldier's energy level could have caused an earthquake."

"What does this mean?" One of the top officials questioned the doctor.

"It means that if we can decide to use these gifts that Seth Phoenix has, and we'd be deliberately reckless not to, we can end this war on terrorism right here and right now. Do you understand what I am telling you?"

"You're telling us that this soldier can change our entire strategy?" General Monroe was stunned and still uncertain.

"I am saying that this soldier has the capabilities that we've been seeking for almost two decades. The visual cortex of this man's brain-that part of the brain that processes visual stimuli- spiked off the charts during a telepathic testing session. We had him wired from eyelash to asshole. And the electromagnetic brain waves that he gave off in a relaxed state were enough to wipe out the stats of any remote viewer that has come before him."

Just then, Seth Phoenix knocked on the door.

Dr. O'Connor turned and looked through the peephole. "It's Seth."

The doctor opened the door and invited Seth to enter. Seth made his way into the room. The tension in the room was almost strangulating as all eyes followed Seth.

"I told you to wait for e, Soldier." Dr. O'Connor studied him.

"I apologize, Doc. But I know what you were discussing. And I need to be at that airport tomorrow, Sir. I need to be there."

CHAPTER 6

Three hours later, Seth Phoenix lay still beneath the cool sheets of his bed. A full night's rest had been forced on him, but it was for his own good and the good of the operation. Sleep deprivation was an enemy. Without ample sleep, his powers would be diminished to those of an average human being. He would be needed the following day, as he would be expected to stop a major terrorist attack on the United States, one that could impact the entire world and would simultaneously mean the slaughtering of hundreds of civilians.

He slowly roused from a deep slumber. He turned on his left side as he fluffed the pillow and breathed deeply. Just as he had settled, something disturbed his consciousness, and his eyes suddenly flew open. He jumped up from his resting position, causing the mattress to bounce as he sat up and stared directly ahead. He realized that he was in a different room, one adjacent to the main lab. He had been brought here to sleep while being monitored, but he knew something was happening in his psyche.

He remained stiff and unable to move as he glanced around the room. Visions darted in and out of his mind, playing fast as if a movie reel was spinning. He was seeing tomorrow. Through the tunnels of his subconscious mind, he was seeing twenty-four hours into the future. Dozens of soldiers were entering the airport, but not because of a suspected terrorist attack. These were soldiers who were on military deployment.

Seth slid his legs across the cool sheets and inched his feet over the side as he pulled himself up and sat on the edge of the bed. He placed his hands on both sides of his head and focused as he slipped into a transient state. He was now viewing tomorrow's victims. He watched as the travelers in the airport moved about, unaware of the terrorist moving among them. He looked like everyone else. There were no warning signs or cautionary announcements. While everyone went about their day-to-day business, they had no idea that the brink of hell was only moments away.

Seth began humming. It was his method and means of comforting himself when he experienced precognition and the terror it sometimes brought, forcing him to decide what knowledge to share. To share or not to share the precognitive Intel was a battle between what was easy and what was ultimately right. He sang the lyrics of a familiar song softly to himself as he massaged the temples, now tender with a dull, throbbing ache.

There in the recesses of his mind's eye were two people. Two people whom he had protected all of his life. As he viewed them in horror, he could see them being dragged to an open field. Their clothes were almost torn completely from their bodies, and their faces were painted with deep lacerations as trickles of blood seeped from the open wounds.

Seth Phoenix snatched the taped wires away from his chest and arms. He jumped to his feet and began pacing the floor. The equipment in the room began to vibrate as he grew increasingly agitated. He was seeing a future event, but how far into the future? Was it a few hours or a few days?

Seth jerked the door open and raced down the hall toward the entrance to the lab. The entire section of the compound was quiet and almost desolate except for three or four people still at work in the main lab. Seth rushed in, just as two remote viewers were preparing to enter a session.

"Where's Dr. O'Connor? I thought he'd be here." Seth's tone was frantic.

Just then, Dr. O'Connor entered the room. "I'm here, Sergeant Major. What the hell is going on?" The monitors in the lab emitted a loud, incessant beeping that echoed throughout the main hall.

"I'm having more visions. I'm seeing tomorrow, or maybe it is only a few hours away. Hell, I don't know. But I know that it's the future."

The doctor pointed Seth to a chair. "Just stay calm, Sergeant Major."

"No, you don't understand. I'm seeing people. Specific people."

"Who?" The doctor stood frozen, unable to move as he listened to Seth.

It's my family, Sir. I saw Abigail and Stephen Phoenix, Sir."

The doctor stared and remained quiet.

"It's my mother and father. They're going to kill my mother and father, along with countless others. And there are at least four dozen soldiers getting on a plane from that airport tomorrow. It's a platoon that's being deployed. I'm seeing all of the victims in the attack."

The doctor nodded. His demeanor was calm and determined as he walked to a landline phone hanging on a wall near the door. He picked up the receiver and dialed the CIA.

The phone rang on the main switchboard operator in the front of the CIA. It was past normal daily operating hours, but in the wake of what lay ahead, the director and top officials remained steadfast in their discussion and planning within a top-secret meeting area of the agency.

Security personnel answered the main line and noted the call location on the monitoring system. A blue, purplish screen highlighted yellow veins on an Earth map, indicating the specific area from which the call was coming. It alerted the guard to the call's supreme importance. The operator recognized the incoming call as Star Gate, the secret underground research laboratory and fallout shelter known only to a few people within the CIA. The operation's existence was kept so secret that anyone calling into the agency was required to use a specific code when dialing out of the bunker. Certain key people at the agency were taught how to recognize when Star Gate was calling. And because of the rarity of receiving phone calls from the compound, it almost always implied that intelligence had been obtained, intelligence that indicated an imminent threat to national security. And it almost always meant that it was happening in real time. Immediate action was imperative. Lost minutes, even seconds, could mean a catastrophe of epic proportions.

The doctor announced his identity as soon as the CIA operator answered the line. "Dr. O'Connor speaking. Get me the director, please."

A couple of minutes passed before the familiar voice of the CIA's director answered the phone. "Dr. O'Connor? This is John Deutch."

The doctor didn't waste time with the usual formalities. "I have new intel from one of our viewers. A very unique viewer. I need to see you immediately. And I need to bring him with me."

"You must mean Sergeant Major Phoenix. You want to bring your new agent here? Why? General Monroe briefed me when he was brought to the lab." Director John Deutch asked.

"So, you know of his capabilities?" Dr. O'Connor asked. The doctor was slightly surprised that Monroe had already notified the CIA. Wasn't that his responsibility?

"From Monroe's documentation. Yes." The director assured him.

The doctor shook his head and paused. "We have a 'Gabriel', John."

The director felt a chilling tingle crescendo throughout his body. His mouth dropped open as he leaned back in his chair.

The doctor noticed his stunned silence. "Are you still there?"

The director mumbled. "Yes."

"I'll say it again in case you didn't hear me." The doctor spoke each word deliberately, as if each word were its own sentence. "We. Have. A. Gabriel."

The director cleared his throat. He spoke low, barely above a whisper, but firm in the delivery. "I will meet you at the NSA. It's closer to you at Fort Meade, and I don't want Phoenix off that base. Yes, definitely, get Phoenix over there. Take Hall C when you get to the Visitor's Center. Take a left when you see the NSA insignia. Then, on your immediate right, push against the side wall, the one with Clinton's picture. You'll see the retina scan. Someone will meet you. And make damn sure no one else sees you two coming in."

Director Deutch hung up the phone and hurried back to the room where he prepared himself to make the announcement to his team. Star Gate, the military's most guarded clandestine operation, had a "Gabriel".

The unmarked armored SUV rolled through the entrance gate to Fort Meade, where Dr. O'Connor and Seth Phoenix were met by three heavily armed soldiers. The soldiers motioned for them to drive forward, and as the vehicle circled the campus, Seth Phoenix took notice of its enormity. Thousands of acres housed Fort Meade, with the National Security Agency resting on almost a hundred acres. The building that housed the Visitor's Complex featured a two-story atrium with a passageway to the meeting hall where Seth and Dr. O'Connor would be going. The building resembled a cube with dark-stained exterior windows. It was a paramount sight to behold, and for a moment, Seth Phoenix felt a twinge of intimidation.

Minutes later, they found themselves standing in front of a retina-scanning device, securely fastened to the wall of the secret inner hallway labeled Hall C, which led to another classified location within the building. And just as the CIA's Director, John Deutch, had promised, the sergeant major and the doctor were met by a security officer who escorted them to a private room where the country's most classified military strategies and Intel operations in the world were being discussed at that very moment.

CHAPTER 7

Seth Phoenix leaned in close enough to almost be touching the black box that was secured against the wall as he waited for the identity scan to complete. A quick flash indicated that his retina had been recognized, his identity confirmed, and he was approved for entry. Dr. O'Connor followed, pressing his eyes against the black box as the scan confirmed his identity. He pulled hard at the door in front of them that would lead them into a secret room that looked more like a chamber. As the men entered the room, the chatter immediately ceased, and all eyes turned toward Seth.

Seth acknowledged the military officers in the room with a salute. Dr. O'Connor motioned for him to sit across from the CIA Director, John Deutch, and the FBI Director of the Counterterrorism Division, Steven Pomerantz. Seth took a seat. He quickly scanned the room, noticing the other men among him and seated at the table. His extrasensory powers instantaneously picked up on the titles of each man, and if he'd had any doubt, he knew then that he was surrounded by some of the most powerful top officials in the U.S. Department of Justice.

"Sergeant Major Phoenix, are you prepared to do whatever we need you to do for the sake of national security?" Director Deutch wasted no time, initiating pertinent questions and directing them to the sergeant major.

"Yes, sir. "I am," Seth answered without any hesitation.

"You understand that we're dealing with a special situation now that we have knowledge of your capabilities." It was less of a question than a statement. The director's gaze was deliberate and now fixed on Seth Phoenix. Their eyes were locked.

"Yes, sir. I have guarded my secret for my entire life, secluding myself from others when necessary. Now, I am a potential threat or a potential savior to the entire world. It's a hell of a place to find yourself." Seth tried to calm down as he quietly took longer, deeper breaths. Dr. O'Connor noticed Seth's hands as he clenched his left fist and then massaged them as if he were attempting to wipe away the anxiety.

"What the hell were you doing all this time back in Tennessee? Before you joined the military?" Chief of Staff of the United States Army, General Gordon Sullivan, leaned forward and aimed his question at Seth from three chairs away.

"Construction. Some residential, but mostly commercial construction."

"So, you are a builder?"

"Yes, sir. And I helped my dad with the farm."

The CSA General Sullivan continued his questioning. "How long have you known that you had these special powers?"

Dr. O'Connor cleared his throat and spoke up, interrupting the interrogation. "I have the sergeant major's medical test results, and they proved--"

The CIA director raised his index finger, halting the doctor's contribution to the discussion. "Let the sergeant major speak, Dr. O'Connor. I trust your findings. However, I am interested in what he has to say."

The doctor nodded. He looked at Seth, who waited to continue.

"I've known since I was about three years old, Sir. But my most vivid memory is when I was on the ball field and couldn't decide whether I was a left-handed batter or a right-handed batter."

The men all responded with a brief smile, and some with a chuckle, acknowledging a familiar scene from their childhood. The room quickly resumed its air of formality, and the sense of urgency returned as the FBI Director Pomerantz tapped on the table.

"We have to get moving, Gentlemen. Sergeant Major Phoenix, what can you tell me about this next terrorist attack? We need any specific details, please. Can you provide us with the terrorist's movements prior to today and up to the present? Director Pomerantz zeroed in on Phoenix.

Seth adjusted himself in his chair and took a deep breath before speaking. His tone was steady and articulate as he described the upcoming scene.

"Our terrorist is living in a middle-income neighborhood just outside of Atlanta. White or cream-colored siding. Ranch-style house. Black shutters on the windows. It's located on a paved street. I see a street sign nearby. The house is on the corner. There's a lot of foot traffic in and out of this house. Probably at least 10 people are coming and going. He has help. He won't be acting alone in the attack."

The men in the room sat rigid. No one was able to move as they listened to Seth provide visual details about the terrorist's location, details that their Intel had already provided to the group. Yet Seth, within seconds of being questioned, was able to describe a scene which he had no reason to know about.

"Are there only ten people?" The FBI director was eager to have questions answered to help him set up a surprise takedown.

"That's about right. Wait. I am seeing inside the house. Damn." Seth leaned forward in his chair and placed his hands on his head. He massaged his temples as he felt the familiar surge of energy through his entire body. The bottom of his feet tingled as the chair began to vibrate.

The men, unfamiliar with this reaction or what might occur in the process, now began backing their chairs away from the table. The FBI director stood up. "What the fuck is going on?"

Dr. O'Connor placed a hand on Seth's shoulder in an attempt to calm him.

"What is it, Sergeant Major? What do you see?" Dr. O'Connor insisted.

"The fucking house is full of explosives and ammo. Judging by the amount, it would be too dangerous to take these bastards in the house. No way to safely barricade them inside there. We have to get them outside of the house, but we have to get them before they launch a suicide bombing. All of them."

"Can you take them out if we get you close enough? The FBI director was about to introduce Seth Phoenix to the FBI's elite. They were the best of the best, most of them being recruits from Army Special Forces units who had completed their four-year enlistment.

Seth gave the director a questioning look and then broke into a slight grin. He nodded, thinking about his humming habit every time he was forced to use telekinesis. He then asked, "Can I sing when I take them out?"

"Sing?" General Monroe interrupted, annoyed by Seth's attempt to find humor, even if it was an attempt intended to ease his tension. The FBI director looked at Monroe.

"Sergeant Major, we don't give a fuck if you whistle *Dixie*. I believe you know what we mean. We want you to take these motherfuckers out the same way that I witnessed you taking that piece of shit out back at Fort Bragg."

Seth Phoenix nodded once. "Yes, sir."

A collective chatter once again filled the room as a sense of certain disaster loomed. The mission had now reached a critical point. The men conversed among themselves as they came to a unanimous conclusion.

The Director of the FBI leaned back and pushed his chair away from the table as he stood up. "Gentlemen, we have a unit sitting on "go" right now. But as you know, the circumstances are highly complex. The sergeant major here didn't provide us with any Intel we didn't already know. So, the real question is, how the hell did he know about it from 650 miles away? Get your people on the phone immediately and advise them that we have a highly classified special agent that will be joining the mission in Atlanta."

Seth sat very quietly. He waited. His breathing was steady. His heart seemed larger as its pulse beat beneath his chest, which suddenly seemed so frail in comparison. He heard the familiar humming of an airplane engine and knew that he was about to board one within the hour.

"Get a plane over here now." The FBI Director pointed at Seth Phoenix. "And get him on it."

Dr. O'Connor started for the door, followed by the other officers. Director Deutch with the CIA intercepted and stopped both him and Seth as Dr. O'Connor reached for the door handle.

The director spoke low, almost in a whisper, and directed his question at Seth. "Sergeant Major, how much do you know about our Star Gate program?"

Seth stood very still and studied the director. He noticed an underlying tone in his question. It was cautionary, a warning that must be heeded. He understood without a doubt that this operation must be kept top secret under any circumstances.

Seth answered firmly. "I don't know anything, Sir."

Dr. O'Connor looked on, observing the director and Seth, waiting for the director to respond to Seth or to release them to go. The director just nodded, silently acknowledging Seth's affirmation, and reached past them for the door handle. He walked past the two men with a commanding presence.

Without turning back, he spoke over his shoulder and left no denying what he meant through the implication of his stern tone. "That's exactly what I expect you to say, Sergeant Major." The door slammed behind him.

CHAPTER 8

0900 hours, Atlanta

Sergeant Major Seth Phoenix hid underneath a dark, starless night sky. A row of shrubbery and flowering trees provided him with just enough obscurity from view to prevent him from being seen by any passersby on the street or anyone who might be looking out from indoors. He crouched down, positioning himself against the warm, grassy earth within a hundred yards of the target: a one-story house with black shutters that was set inconspicuously on the corner. Several men within the Al Qaeda terrorist ring had already entered the house. They were recruits; ordinary American citizens who had been brainwashed by an extremist and psychopathic regime determined to destroy and kill innocent people.

Within seconds, Seth was surrounded by FBI special agents who were also staying hidden and who were now preparing to raid the house. A dozen soldiers of the Army's Delta Force had also been deployed to the mission but hung back from where the FBI special agents and Seth kept hiding, awaiting further instruction from the commander in charge. Seth had been positioned at the forefront because of his abilities, an advantage that the enemy had no way of conquering. He could hear their conversations in detail and could even smell the food that they were eating from his position a hundred yards away. And, if necessary, he could disarm and disable any or all of them before they could harm any member of his unit.

Seth crouched low and remained dead still while watching from his hiding place and keeping his mind homed in on the house and the activities inside. A sudden, excruciating pain sliced across his neck, causing him to grab his throat. Because of his supernatural abilities and the fact that there was no actual cut or blood, he immediately knew that he was experiencing an empathetic response to the pain of someone else, someone who would be arriving at the property at any minute. Still in a crouching position, Seth slowly crawled backward, careful not to be seen as cars turned the corner at the entrance of the neighborhood. Although the headlights shone brightly on him each time a vehicle passed, he remained invisible. Two of the agents positioned close to Seth noticed his movement. They remained quiet as they kneeled close to the ground and moved toward him. The only way they could communicate with each other was a hand signal, as Seth quickly motioned for them to gather close.

Seth moved fast as he crawled across the grass, barren ground that stained his clothes with brown dirt and clumps of sticky mud from a three-day-old rain shower. He reached the other team members and took a deep breath. His voice was barely above a whisper, but there was no mistaking the grave tone.

"In a few minutes, a vehicle is going to arrive at the house. Inside the vehicle is an individual who has been kidnapped. The group plans to video an execution for propaganda."

The men stared at the sergeant major with what could only be perceived as pure determination to seize or to kill, if necessary, every member of the terrorist cell who was hiding inside the house; a house situated among other modest American homes where families were completely oblivious to what was transpiring within their very own neighborhood, and for some, right next door.

"We have to stop this. It's now or never. I mean, the bastards are right here in the middle of goddamn suburbia. If they get wind that we're here, the shit will hit the fan, for sure. And we're not talking, just a gun fight. As I've already told you, they've got enough ammo and explosives inside that house to level two city blocks. It'll be a fucking war zone." Seth's adrenaline was kicked into overdrive as he explained to the other agents in his company and then paused. He mulled over the situation some more. What would it take for him to disable them, he wondered? And if he managed to rescue the hostage, what kind of demonstration of power would it spark from the cell inside?

"Son of a Bitch. I've got to call this in." Jim Garcia, the FBI commander in charge of the operation, spoke with authority and determination. He brushed away a film of gritty sand that had managed to get into his eyes while stepping away from the team. He turned and headed in a direction for privacy.

Minutes later, he rejoined the sergeant major and all remaining members of the team. They hurriedly gathered together in a remote area adjacent to the opening of the neighborhood, even though they were still only a couple of hundred yards away from the target.

Agent Jim Garcia softly gave a birdcall, signaling the rest of the men to listen up. He spoke fast and firmly as he gave instructions for moving in.

The Army Special Forces Unit, composed of eight men, was now repositioned to cover Sergeant Major Phoenix as he maneuvered closer to the house. They would enter the house after Seth managed to rescue the hostage from the clutches of Al Qaeda, before they were able to get the hostage inside. A surprise rush would eliminate the terrorist's ability to detonate any explosives or fire any weapons. The SF team would stand steady in formation while covering the FBI team and the sergeant major. The idea was a fast-and-furious approach.

As Jim concluded his instructions, he paused for a moment to confirm that all understood. "Everybody got that?"

Whispers could be heard among a few of the men. They were doubtful. The assignment had suddenly turned into a search-and-rescue mission based on the intel Seth Phoenix had just provided to them. But it was Intel that the entire team wasn't completely confident with. Seth Phoenix had the support of Dr. O'Connor and several top officials within the U.S. Department of Justice, but they knew about Star Gate. They knew the reality of who he was and what he could do, and this was no game; now he was playing for real. He was standing among some of the most highly trained badasses in the United States military and the FBI's elite. Now wasn't the time to decide who was on the right side or what the mission was meant to accomplish. At that moment, an FBI agent stepped forward.

"Sir, ten minutes ago, we were prepared to rush this place and take these assholes out. Now you're telling us that we have to wait for a hostage to show up. How do we know this?"

Seth Phoenix felt the tension rising in the group. He slowly eased aside and stood a few steps away from the conversation. The commanding agent, Jim Garcia, nodded in acknowledgment but did not offer to back down from his position.

"Gentlemen, the orders have been given. Sergeant Major Phoenix will assume a post within a few feet of the target's driveway. You will get the signal to storm the residence as soon as Phoenix has control of the hostage situation. The SF units will provide support and take out any of those scumbags who even look like they have metal in their hands."

The silence that resonated among the men seemed to further deepen the already grave, grim tone of the night. Nothing that had been said up to this point had worked to dispel any of the team's doubts. That is, nothing until Seth Phoenix confronted the team and Agent Garcia with a would-be revelation that would lift the veil of uncertainty to provide them all with an unequivocal validation.

Seth stood in the center of the men. He looked over at Agent Garcia's face, which was now dimly lit and thereby visible from the illuminating ray of a flashlight beam. "Tell them, Sir. Tell them who changed the orders."

Agent Garcia stared at Seth, hesitating for a moment before responding, but then, as he spoke, he placed a great deal of emphasis on every word. "Gentlemen, our orders are coming straight from the *White House*."

A vehicle turned the corner and proceeded down the street toward the target residence. Seth Phoenix began stalking the vehicle's movement as his eyes scanned it over. He mentally gathered information about the people inside, processing it like a hard drive, recording data at lightning speed. The hostage was male. Some sort of minister of faith. A small crucifix hung around his neck. He was fatigued and sat slouched down in the front seat, his head leaning back. However, Seth could make out trickles of blood zigzagging across the hostage's face. One of the assailants sat in the rear seat with a .45 caliber handgun resting against the minister's head.

Seth prepared for immediate action, aligning his energy reserves with his supernatural source. While his eyes were steady on the vehicle, he caused his body temperature to climb through mental manipulation. His metabolism began to speed up, and he felt the familiar tingling in his hands and feet as the sensation traveled down his body. It was like watching a kettle of water begin to boil. Once his energy level reached the necessary crescendo, there was no stopping the surge that would ultimately be expelled from his body. He took deep breaths and began to hum what he had now labeled as the 'Seth Phoenix Soundtrack' tune. It was his proven method of calming and controlling his "gift".

Seth heard the minister's suffering laments from within the car. The minister grimaced as the terrorist pulled his head back against the seat. Seth could feel his pain. His thoracic region was heavily battered and bruised. Ribs were fractured or possibly broken. Each time the minister took a breath, he winced as agonizing pain ripped through his body. Seth mumbled to himself. *Motherfuckers. That's what they are. Senseless. Barbaric. Sadist Bastards.*

The vehicle pulled to a stop in the drive. Seth's body literally vibrated as he watched. He was posted on the driveway, just a few feet from the vehicle. Keeping his calm was crucial at this point. He had to wait until he could see the hostage outside the car before he reacted. The FBI was now in a position to storm the target. At this point, everything appeared to move in slow motion as the terrorists dragged the minister from the car.

A look of horror came over the minister's face as the assailants began to pummel his head with their fists, laughing in unison with each strike. They pushed him to the ground and ordered him to stand up and walk. Dust and dirt stirred as the minister stumbled to his feet. His wrists were covered in blood from the tightness and burning of the rope that was used to secure his hands behind his back.

Seth was now able to determine exactly what weapons the terrorists were holding. It appeared that both men were carrying an AK-47, but one of the terrorists was using a Glock .45 caliber handgun while the rifle was strapped around his neck. Seth moved quickly and into clear view of the hostage as he projected his energy field directly forward. He held his arms out in front of him, propelling an invisible force at the two men standing directly behind the hostage. He aimed for their backs as he unleashed a violent hammering impact against them. The men screamed out as they collapsed on their knees. They grasped at their backs in vain, unable to determine what had caused the crushing sensation that now rippled along their ribcages.

Seth made direct eye contact with the two terrorists as they slowly turned around to face him. Their confusion and angst were evident on their faces as they stared back. Seth looked deep into their eyes, dark pools of evil. It was darkness unlike anything he had ever encountered, a cold black iris that seemed to be the window to a demon's soul. They reached for their weapons that had fallen by their sides upon the hammering impact and pointed them directly at Seth, but his energy force surrounded them from all sides. Holding his position steady by the vehicle, Seth watched as the hostage fell to the ground and began crawling away from the area where the two terrorists now sat hunched over and pointing their guns. He maintained control of the terrorists as he continued to send ripples of shock waves directly at and through their bodies, causing them to convulse as if they were being electrocuted. Suddenly, the terrorists grabbed their ears just as their eardrums burst, releasing a violent ejaculation of blood that trickled down the sides of their neck.

Just then, the FBI unit saw Seth make a sudden rush for the hostage. That was the signal that they'd been waiting for, and the unit pushed forward toward the house. The breechers swiftly planted the explosives in the door frame of the house and rushed out of the way. The first entry man detonated the bomb, blowing the front entrance door into nothing more than tiny slivers of wood. The detonation sounded like a thousand slamming doors as smoke swirled around the entrance for a moment. The men were lightning fast as they busted through the front door. Just then, Seth heard shouting and screams coming from the house. Chaos and confusion. He grabbed the back of the minister's coat and turned him around so that the minister's left arm could be placed around his neck as he rushed him to safety. Seth reached a low-lying ditch nearby and placed the minister on the ground, shielding him from gunfire or a possible blast.

Then Seth turned his attention back to the house. The SF Team, still positioned outside and across the street from the house, was now being targeted as one of the terrorists held a gun outside a front window, scattering bullets in every direction as he fired the AK-47. Inside the house, the FBI stepped over the bodies of seven men who had met their fate just seconds before.

But the one man still alive inside was now barricaded in a front room that was full of explosives, including a stash of hand grenades. He strapped a row of them onto his body and laced his fingers through the pins.

Seth Phoenix stood frozen as he watched a mental visualization develop before his eyes of the assailant and the FBI agents still inside the front main room of the dwelling. Words flashed through his mind like huge flashcards. Just then, the familiar popping sound of a gunshot paralyzed him, and he knew that time was up. Not even a second of hesitation was acceptable; there was no time to consider the consequences of utilizing his supernatural abilities, as mental images, one after the other, flashed through his mind, ordering him to act now! He stepped forward and faced the front of the house, concentrating with the tenacity of a neurosurgeon as he mentally blocked out all interference from his hearing range. He visually zeroed in on the lone terrorist in the front window with the intention of physically stopping him from pulling the pins out of the grenades. With the strength of his energy, he now focused his efforts on moving each finger, one by one if necessary.

Shouts echoed over the secret radio frequency between the FBI agents inside the house and the SF team members outside as the SF ordered the FBI to hurry out.

"Abort, abort! Get the fuck out of there! Get out! Get out now!" The shouts were in unison as the FBI agents inside the house rushed to the front door.

Seth Phoenix stood still, facing the house, homed in on the lone terrorist whose fingers were still positioned in the pins. Although he was dressed in full body armor, an explosion of this proportion would certainly kill him and take out any of the agents within blast range. A pulsating energy began to envelop him, acting as an invisible armor as he attempted to get closer to the terrorist.

Agent Garcia could see Seth from a short distance and knew that he was trying to get closer to the house. The commander began shouting at the sergeant major to abort. "Phoenix, get your ass back here!"

Seth continued forward, relatively unaware of any external distractions, as he focused with a sharp, indomitable intent to cease and then destroy. And this time it had to be done by different means, unlike any he had ever used before. Because the terrorist already had his fingers positioned on the pins, ready to yank them from the hand grenades and blow up the whole block, Seth had to use the most powerful and effective of his supernatural capabilities. And he must act very quickly so that the assailant wouldn't have time to react and pull any of the pins. With a combined audience of thirty-seven SF units and FBI agents, Seth Phoenix had no other choice but to unveil the extent of his power. From a distance of forty feet away, he would stop the terrorist's heart from beating. And with the terrorist's fingers tightly grasping the pins, he had to do it at once.

CHAPTER 9

An eerie silence seemed to suspend time as Seth Phoenix stood in place, rigid and calm. He examined the area with his peripheral vision and watched the scene unfold like a slow-motion reel. Two FBI units had dragged the two bloody terrorists away and cuffed them. Everything seemed to be happening in a supercharged time warp where seconds fell away faster than the speed of light, but Seth was locked in a slow-motion frame.

The last remaining terrorist watched from the corner of the window, stalking Seth Phoenix as he waited for Seth to get closer to the house. Seth stopped within ten feet and managed to lock eyes with the terrorist. He assessed the situation and now knew that stopping the terrorist's heart would have to be completed by way of a direct kill. At this vantage point, the terrorist was now within Seth's telekinetic reach, enabling him to mentally project a bullet of energy straight for the terrorist's head.

Seth straightened his body, breathed in deeply, and, drawing from the energy that surged again within him, aimed a massive discharge of power toward the window. His cheeks throbbed as that energy evolved with immense, forceful propulsion. His eyes manipulated the movement of the energy as he guided the telekinetic bullet straight for the terrorist's left eye socket. For a split second, he noticed the man flinch as if he suddenly sensed the rapid deliverance of his death. But the terrorist had no time to react as the invisible bullet entered his head, splitting a portion of his cerebellum in half. He slumped back from the window and fell with a hard thud against the wood floor, blood gushing from what was left of his now severed head. Seth watched from a distance, still using his spatial sense to view the area around him. And as the last terrorist fell, all eyes became fixed on him.

Every team member's gaze was intense as they studied the secret weapon the military had unveiled. But Seth Phoenix had made a mistake. He was supposed to be the team's tool for providing supernatural Intel. Not a supernatural weapon that, just by his mere existence alone, eliminated the need for the most advanced government weaponry. This was a mistake he was sure he had made. And couldn't they have known? Shouldn't someone have thought this out? If the situation changed and Seth Phoenix or any of his team members were suddenly in harm's way, didn't they know he would act again to protect himself or them? If the United States Military wanted to keep him a safely guarded secret, they would have to find a way to use him from a remote location. Placing Seth Phoenix at the target site was like provoking an uncaged lion. His response would not be contained. And yet, was that their intention all along?

The neighborhood suddenly became illuminated as curious people flicked on their porch lights after hearing faint gunshots from a quarter mile away. The commander whispered loudly while motioning for Seth to hurry away from the area.

Local law enforcement was supposed to handle the scene and provide a cover-up story for the media. No one needed to know just yet about Al Qaeda living in the suburbs of Atlanta.

"Get the fuck out of here. Move!" Garcia pointed toward the nearby house. Someone was awake.

Seth heard the faint sound of footsteps shuffling across the grass in the distance as team members raced to exit the site. They made a fast retreat toward the trees where their unmarked vehicles were waiting, along with the van that now held the terrorists in shackles and chains. The men jumped into the seats and slammed the doors shut, and a nearby neighbor heard the engines accelerate as they departed the area.

Back in Washington, D.C.

The phone rang incessantly until finally CIA Director John Deutch rolled over and slammed his hand against the nightstand. He fumbled for the receiver and swung his legs over the side of the bed as he sat up, gripping the receiver in his right hand.

"Hello." He cleared his throat and rubbed his eyes. Telephone calls at three a.m. were never a good sign.

"This is Pomerantz. I need to talk to you, but not over the phone."

The director sighed and waited for further instructions.

"Star Gate 3-3-0."

"Yeah." The director hung up. He quickly dressed and then tiptoed out of the room, careful not to make any noise. The soles of his shoes were relatively silent on the plush carpet. The

Mrs. was still sleeping soundly, and thereby unsuspecting her husband's urgent departure. As the director walked into the kitchen, he stopped and opened a dish cabinet. He grabbed a large mug and poured it full of cold coffee that was left over from the morning. He placed the mug in the microwave for thirty seconds, then opened the back door and exited through the garage.

The night sky looked no different than on any other night, and the usual humming sound of 18- wheelers roaring past on the nearby highway sent the director into a sort of trance, as though he was momentarily suspended in time. He thought about the call he'd just received and what message he would be receiving within a few minutes. Phone calls in the middle of the night had historical significance. After spending his entire career working for the government, at least in some capacity, either as a military officer or currently as the head of the CIA, late-night phone calls were a dreaded part of the territory. But it almost always meant that hell had just broken loose.

Once in his car and on the road, he drove quickly to Star Gate headquarters. He was being summoned to receive and discuss classified information. But this was different. This was more than just the usual classified discussion. He could sense that something else was wrong. The director took the next exit and pulled off the main highway. He drove for about a mile and then turned onto an unmarked, paved street that twisted and wound into a dusty, gravel road after a two-mile trek. Finally, the car reached the dead-end trail leading to the underground lab.

He parked among a group of trees and waited for military security personnel to approach and escort him to the hidden door. With stealth precision, a heavily armed military soldier stepped from out of nowhere, it seemed and motioned to the director to proceed toward the stairs that led to the main underground entrance.

"Good morning, Sir." The soldier greeted the director, extended his hand, and signaled for the director to walk in front of him. Once he reached the bottom of the stairs, he reached for the door handle after passing the retina scan but was startled as the door suddenly pushed open. Dr. O'Connor had been anxiously waiting for his arrival. The director noticed the obvious distress Dr. O'Connor was feeling in the doctor's expressions. His skin was pale and ashen, and his forehead was covered in worry lines.

"We're all here." Dr. O'Connor announced their intention to get started at once.

The director only responded with a nod as he made his way to the conference area. He entered the room and took a seat. He wiped his hand over his face in an effort to wake himself.

"Ok, Doc. What the hell is going on?"

FBI Director Pomerantz spoke up. "We were informed just a few hours ago that we have a mole on the inside."

"We what? Who? How?"

"Someone has leaked Sergeant Major Seth Phoenix's identity to a Russian agent."

"God Almighty." The room filled with whispers as the men weighed in on this development, their voices rising to a loud chatter.

"You're telling me that this sergeant major, whom we just met a few days ago, is now on the damn hotwire to Russia?" CIA Director Deutch was irate.

"Someone saw him back at the base before he ever got to Fort Meade. It had to originate from there. We suspect that the mole has already passed along his identity and his ability." Pomerantz said.

"How do we know this?" The director leaned forward.

"One of our informants in Moscow sent a message that a large sum of money was being transferred to an American bank account in exchange for military records." Pomerantz's expression was tense, his tone grave.

Where is Phoenix now?" The director asked. His eyes appeared bleak as he made eye contact with Pomerantz.

"He's en route here. He and his team just finished the task outside of Atlanta. They also managed to intercept a kidnapping/hostage situation. They rescued a minister who was about to be executed on camera."

The director's eyes twitched and his face screwed up as he meditated on this information, drawing strength from his unwavering desire and determination to conquer terrorism within the United States' home boundaries. Sleeper cells were now operating in all states across America. The media's estimate of three to four thousand hidden operatives was well off the mark. With more than seventeen thousand Al Qaeda operatives in the United States, the probability of another major attack on U.S. soil was mounting as seconds ticked by.

Suddenly, a knock at the door caused the room to fall silent, and all eyes shifted toward the door. As the men stood, a uniformed military security officer entered the room and wasted no time in delivering his message. He stood in front of the FBI Director Pomerantz, who locked eyes with him while the CIA Director Deutch stood by his side.

"Sir, there is a media frenzy going down outside these walls. CNN News is on the phone. They know about Atlanta."

"God damnit," Deutch shouted and clenched his fists as a sinking feeling came over him. He looked around the room at the faces of the other men. No one uttered a word as they all studied each other in mutual contemplation. The situation was rapidly spinning out of control. And time was running out.

"Hold them off." Deutch gave his order and nodded for the officer to exit the room. He took a breath and hesitated for a moment. He glanced around the room that had fallen silent and knew that everyone realized what was at stake. They all sat dead still, almost stoic as they waited for him to provide further direction.

They knew that the most guarded and top-secret United States Military Intel program was about to become a global news sensation. They had guarded Star Gate and its headquarters with bravery and loyalty to the operation for almost two decades. Even in its dormancy after Ronald Reagan left office, a select few had fought to preserve it. And now, after finding a "Gabriel", a superhuman capable of validating the research of two decades, the operation was in danger of losing its most vital component, because Seth Phoenix would now be the most hunted man on the planet.

Deutch picked up the receiver from a landline phone on the conference table. The room remained quiet as he pressed the numbers on the phone's keypad. With each key's beep, he could feel his heart thumping as he wiped a hint of sweat from his brow. The phone rang several times at the receiving end before a familiar voice answered. "The White House."

CHAPTER 10

Seth Phoenix climbed aboard the C12 and sat down in a seat near the back of the plane. He sighed and rubbed his hand over his face as he stretched his legs out, positioning them in the aisle, since his six-foot-three-inch frame wouldn't accommodate the close quarters between seats. As the plane's engines began to vibrate, Seth massaged his temples. His dark brown crew cut was streaked with dried sweat and dirt, and his face was still warm from the sudden spiking of his body temperature during the most recent expulsion of telekinetic energy. He was unusually exhausted and needed sleep. He reached inside his front shirt pocket and removed the General's "chill" pill. He tossed the medicine in his mouth and swallowed it with a swish of bottled water that he had grabbed from the drink cooler when he entered the plane. As he leaned back and closed his eyes, thoughts flooded his mind like a raging river, drowning everything in its path. Along with these thoughts came dozens of questions that demanded answers, questions that he had begun to ask himself. Questions such as *Why is this happening now?*

A rush of memories flooded his mind, memories from his childhood. As the plane began to lift off, Seth Phoenix fell backward into his memories, memories that played out like a stage performance, with him now observing his past as an audience member.

He watched his teacher and her assistant writing across the board in his sixth-grade science class. He was bored and sleepy, struggling to stay awake that day. He rubbed his eyes and played with the items on his desk. His notebook was closed until he began flipping the pages open using his telekinetic ability. First, it was one page. Then two or three at a time until suddenly he had the entire notebook of three hundred pages flipping and flapping against each other. He was mesmerized by his own demonstration and wasn't even aware of his teacher and her assistant, or of the other students who had gathered near the front of the class, now watching in fear and awe. Mouths were draped open, and Mrs. Holley was unable to move. She finally managed to shout the words escaping from her lips quickly and in a desperate panic to stop the scene before them, a scene that was frightening to those who didn't understand its future significance.

"Seth! Seth, what are you doing?!" Her voice cracked, and her body trembled as the notebook slammed shut. Seth stared up at her and the others with sudden fear and regret.

"I'm sorry, Mrs. Holley," Seth whispered. His eyes began to moisten with tears as he bent his head down, refusing to look at any of them again.

Mrs. Holley was visibly afraid, her hands trembling as she patted the back of one of the students, urging him to return to his seat. Her speech was shaky, but she had to gain control of the classroom again as she addressed Seth. "Seth, I need you to come with me. Okay?"

The Phoenix Project

Seth Phoenix stood up from his desk and walked to the front of the classroom. Mrs. Holley opened the door and signaled the remaining students, who still stood in awe at the front of the classroom, to return to their empty desks. She glanced at her assistant, whose mouth still hung open and who still had her hand resting on her chest as if she was trying to catch her breath.

The door closed behind them as Seth and Mrs. Holley walked purposefully to the principal's office, where he would be questioned and made to wait in the lobby until his mother was phoned and summoned to the school. He recalled his mother's facial expression as she entered the front office. Her eyes were moist, and her brow furrowed as she walked toward Seth, who was seated on a bench just outside the principal's office. She sat down beside him, comforting him by patting and rubbing his shoulder. The principal summoned them and invited them into his office. Mrs. Phoenix then stood and, without saying a word, walked into the principal's office, shutting the door behind her. She sat down in a seat directly across from him.

Seth just waited alone. He felt an air of relief upon seeing his mother, but he knew this would be a turning point for him. How would others treat him now? Would everyone be scared of him? Although the principal's office door was tightly shut, Seth Phoenix could hear his mother's conversation with an accuracy normally only possible through wiretapping. To the rest of the people in the room, muffled voices were the only sounds they could detect.

He listened intently as Abigail Phoenix disclosed her son's extraordinary birthright. Seth fidgeted in his chair, feeling uncomfortable with his secrets being revealed to school officials. Surely his mother knew when to stop this interrogation. He couldn't just sit there and allow her to tell too much. Besides, he had only used psychokinesis to move a pencil here and there. That was just a parlor trick compared to what he was capable of.

Seth looked around the room, observing the school secretary and other people coming in and out of the front office where he sat. Ms. Holley stood near the inside door of the principal's office as she listened to the discussion. Seth heard his mother telling the principal that her son had managed to teach himself magic tricks. *Thank God. She was trying to defuse the situation by offering a half-truth.* It seemed to work. Although Mrs. Holley still appeared to be stunned by the incredible demonstration she'd witnessed, and the principal was disturbed by what he'd learned from her, they believed Abigail Phoenix because it was logical to do so. Any other explanation would have required pure and absolute acceptance of a paranormal phenomenon beyond human understanding.

On the plane, Seth twisted in his chair, now drifting in and out of sleep. He sat up and propped his chin against the palm of his hand. He silently talked to himself, mouthing words. It was an attempt to calm his thoughts and to essentially make peace with the reality of what had just transpired outside of Atlanta. He drifted back in, his thoughts telling a story aloud within the privacy of his own subconscious, where no one else could hear or be privy to what he was sharing. He had no audience, and it felt safe.

And so, it was in the childhood days of Seth Phoenix, a concealed and misunderstood identity. It haunts me. This is why I wanted to be more than an abnormality. I wanted to belong, and joining the United States Military gave me an opportunity to be a part of something greater than myself. But now he was being forced to use extreme measures in a time dictated by terrorist threats in the homeland and abroad.

A tapping on his shoulder stirred Seth awake from an inconsistent sleep. He came fully awake and alert, his eyes shooting open as he found a soldier standing over him. He stared into the soldier's eyes as the soldier handed a phone to him. "It's for you, Phoenix."

Seth looked down at the phone and slowly raised it to his ear. He opened and closed his eyes several times as he focused on his surroundings. His voice was gruff. "This is Phoenix."

"Sergeant Major." Dr. O'Connor offered a quick greeting.

"Yes, I'm here." Seth immediately recognized the doctor's voice.

"How are your energy levels right now, Sergeant Major?"

"Depleted. Why?"

"Don't you already know?" The doctor was somewhat surprised that Phoenix hadn't already acknowledged the reason for his call.

Seth figured he was calling to congratulate him on the Atlanta takedown. "No. We just killed a house full of fucking terrorists, Doctor, and I'm in metabolic restoration right now." Seth couldn't conceal his irritability from exhaustion.

The doctor paused. On the other side of the phone, he rubbed his face and sighed. He already knew about the takedown. Every agent and soldier there deserved to be awarded a medal for doing a job most people wanted no part of, but now the stakes were steadily rising as he wondered how the hell the U.S. government was going to deal with the threat of having classified information that was meant to protect the American people, shared with the entire world. The doctor mouthed a response without making a sound.

Damn, there's something new to learn about this Seth Phoenix every minute. Metabolic Restoration. Fancy words that could describe any other human on the planet, but not Phoenix. His metabolic restoration is a whole different process that enables him to perform feats of power that no other human being on earth possesses. Ok, got it.

The doctor then spoke in an abrupt, stern manner, unlike his usual tone. "I need you to come clean with me, Sergeant Major. If you are withholding anything, now is the time to bring it out."

"What the hell are you talking about?" Seth wasn't in the mood for another bullshit interrogation.

"I'm talking about Fort Bragg and the attack. Your buddies, Nick and Finley."

"I told you everything that happened, Doctor. What the fuck?" Seth switched the phone to the other side of his head and leaned against the window, shielding his voice from any nearby eavesdropping. The plane was minutes away from landing, and some of the men had started to stir from their in-flight naps.

"Ok, ok. Look, I believe you. But listen to me and listen well. We've got a real fucking problem that just went global, and we're turning over every rock we can find." The doctor's tone was taut.

Seth's breathing and pulse rate began to speed up. He was receiving Intel in the form of visual flashes that flicked rapidly on and off in his head. He could see an outline of a man. Or was he picking up emphatic cues from the doctor?

"I'm getting images right now. What is this about?" Seth spoke in an undertone and glanced around the cabin to make sure the other men were preoccupied and not zeroing in on his conversation.

"We have a mole. And we have reason to believe that he was at Fort Bragg during the attack, that he saw you, and that he saw what happened when you rescued Nick and Finley."

Seth shook his head. "Ok, so?" He began to sweat because he knew what was coming, but maintaining denial felt better at the moment than facing the consequences of using his powers in broad daylight.

"Your identity and your abilities as the new United States Military's top-secret weapon have now been shared with Russia. A Russian spy was among us at the base. And not one of our military personnel or any of our top security officers on the entire fucking two hundred fifty square mile base suspected this bastard might be committing or even capable of espionage."

Seth's face began to feel hot, and he suddenly felt nauseous. "What now?"

"We have a meeting."

Seth shook his head and huffed. "A meeting…?"

"Yes, that's right. A meeting. Get your ass in here as soon as you get off that plane. Two decades of research have just been scattered across the entire goddamn globe. And the fucking CIA just called the president."

CHAPTER 11

As soon as the plane's tires hit the pavement, Seth Phoenix was out of his seat and anxiously waiting near the exit door. His cell phone began to beep. Text messages were flooding his inbox. One right after another. It was Finley.

Need to talk.

Need to talk now, Man.

Answer the damn phone.

Where the fuck are you?

Call me now.

Stop jerking off and call me.

Phoenix, are you my friend?

Seth quickly scrolled through the messages before hitting the phone icon to dial Finley's number. The phone rang several times before the voice messaging system picked up. Seth's fingers raced across the phone's keypad as he typed Finley a message.

Trying to call you.

Been on a plane.

Answer the fucking phone.

Seth dialed Finley again. The voice messaging system answered.

"Son of a bitch. What the hell is going on?" Seth growled through clenched teeth. He closed his eyes and focused on Finley, trying to locate him. Fuzzy. Nothing concrete.

Suddenly, Seth's phone began to buzz with an incoming call. It was Finley. He swiped the phone with his finger, eager to connect, and glanced around the cabin. Finley answered on the other end by only offering a low grunt that sounded like a "hello."

"Hey, Man. What the hell is going on?" Seth's words were clipped.

"I need to talk to you," Finley whispered into the phone.

"Wh-What the hell? Are you okay?"

"Yeah, yeah. But I've been poked and probed nine ways to Sunday, Man. And Nick, too. We're getting our balls busted because these damn guys think we know something about a terrorist cell or an undercover Russian spy. What the fuck?"

Seth paused for a few seconds and thought about what Finley was saying. They were interrogating Finley and Nick because they witnessed his power. They were eyewitnesses, but so was the general.

Seth took a breath. "Finley, who else saw me pull you and Nick out of there?"

"What? I don't know, Man. Nick was hurt. Remember? We both were. We just survived a damn blast that blew the fucking roof away. What are you-?"

"We have a mole." Seth interrupted.

"What? What are you saying? You left right after the attack. Where did they take you?"

"I'm staying in a secret location. I can't give you details. The military is using me for Intel purposes. Where is Nick?"

"The last I knew, he was in the hospital. I haven't seen him since, but I talked to him. He told me that he had been questioned about you."

"Questioned? What kinds of questions?" Seth's tone was forceful.

"The same ones I've gotten. Questions about who you are. How do we know you? How long have we known you? If you have ever shown any supernatural abilities before. Personal questions about ourselves. Seemed like they thought that we also had some type of supernatural ability."

Seth fell silent. He breathed deeply, calming himself. "What did you say?"

Finley shook his head in disbelief and aggravation. "I told them, Hell, yeah, I was Superman- What the fuck do you think I told them? I told them hell, no. I didn't say shit after that, but I damn sure laughed."

"Where are you now?" Seth asked.

Finley whispered into the phone. "Fort Meade."

Seth felt a wave of anxiety wash over his body. "Holy fuck."

"What? What is it, Man?" Finley demanded.

"They're bringing you here." Seth was certain.

"Where? Where the fuck are they bringing me?" Finley was now anxious, but Seth remained quiet. "Phoenix. Man, answer me."

"Relax." Seth paused, gathering his thoughts.

"How the hell am I supposed to relax?"

"I get it now."

Seth glanced behind him and noticed the other team members moving from their seats. "Hey, Finley. I've gotta go, Man. Don't worry. I'll be seeing you in a few hours."

The phone went dead as Finley paused and stared ahead in bewilderment. He let out a sigh and began silently praying for divine protection. War was one thing. He knew who the enemy was when he was in a war zone, but here? He had no idea who the enemy was or even if he was moving to the front line. And what would he be fighting against? His friendship with Seth Phoenix had suddenly labeled him a suspect. Guilty by association. But guilty of what?

One Hour Later at Star Gate Headquarters...

Sergeant Major Seth Phoenix entered the secret underground door after pausing for a retina scan. As he entered the hallway, he saw high-ranking officials already waiting for his arrival. Phoenix raised his hand to salute General Gordon Sullivan, the Chief of Staff of the United States Army. The men followed to the conference room and slammed the door, locking it behind them. In the far-left corner of the room, Finley McCall sat quietly, his eyes searching the faces of everyone who entered.

Seth noticed his friend and inwardly breathed a sigh of relief that he had been brought to the headquarters. He would be safe. At least for now. Once they figured out that Finley didn't know anything, they would release him back to the base, where tensions were high-strung, and no one knew who the enemy was.

Dr. O'Connor motioned for Seth to sit near Finley. Seth studied every person's face in the room, summing up their moods and focusing on their thoughts. The CIA Director Deutch's thoughts were bouncing back and forth like a ping pong ball as he contemplated Finley's guilt. He had his doubts. No one could be trusted at this point. Could Finley be the mole? He was there and witnessed the entire scene. No one else knew about Seth Phoenix. Or did they?

Seth listened as the other men in the room spoke barely above a whisper at the front of the table. *Finley, a possible remote viewer like Phoenix? They would keep him for a couple of days to assess his abilities. Dr. O'Connor would use the program's other remote viewers to assist Phoenix in uncovering who the mole was and where they were. And what Russia was intending to do with the new information.*

Seth invaded Dr. O'Connor's mind. Tapping into hidden information that he had carefully been guarding. Seth fidgeted in his seat and fought the urge to confront the doctor. He lowered his head and pretended not to be interested in the conversation at the front of the table. He kept a cool demeanor and an "I don't give a shit" expression as he gathered information from every man in the room. And at that moment, he became privy to how Star Gate had been born as a top-secret military program. Russia had its own "Seth Phoenix". And *she* had been around for much longer than he had.

CHAPTER 12

Moscow, Russia
The Kremlin

Russian President Boris Yeltsin walked around his 19th-century French Empire-style desk. He stopped and stood in front of a world map hanging on the wall behind his chair. He stared at the mass territory before him and reveled for a moment in the reality of his reign over the world's largest country. A magnificent, gold-framed mirror hung on the opposite wall and reflected the Russian president's thick, lustrous white hair and tall 6'2' frame as he contemplated the latest Intel that he had received.

He placed his hands in his pockets as he waited for the prime minister to arrive with details concerning an irrefutable discovery made by an undercover Russian spy. He had been given the news about an American with supernatural abilities equal to Russia's own psychic spy, known by the code name Nikita Oleshin. She was given the code name, which meant "unconquered defender," by Lieutenant Colonel Vladimir Putin, a top agent in the Russian KGB's foreign intelligence division, and she was the country's top secret Intel instrument providing intelligence to the Russian military and the Kremlin for the past five years through telekinetic means.

Just then, a knock on the door signaled that the prime minister had arrived. The president responded with an order to enter as the prime minister pushed the door open and walked into the room. He extended his right hand, greeting the president with a firm, steady handshake. The men sat down in matching leather chairs facing each other in front of President Yeltsin's desk. The prime minister wasted no time in passing along a peremptory message.

"Mr. President, I've just received confirmation from the SVR that the United States has an individual within the United States Army who matches our Nikita."

The president's eyes, which were focused on the colors of the carpet beneath his feet, now quickly locked with the prime minister's stare. The expression on the men's faces revealed what each was thinking. The president paused for a moment. The SVR was Russia's Foreign Intelligence Service.

And is this information trustworthy? How do we know?"

"He witnessed the man's power. It was at Fort Bragg, Sir. In North Carolina."

The president rubbed his finger across his chin as he processed what he was being told. "Fort Bragg. The terrorist attack just a few days ago. It was there."

"That's correct, Mr. President. Al Qaeda was behind the attack, but our spy witnessed him move a roomful of debris off of two soldiers who had been hit during the explosion."

"Who is he? What do we know about him?"

"Sergeant Major Seth Phoenix. He's with the—

The president shook his head and leaned forward. "Tell me again. Where did this information come from? The SVR?"

"What do you mean? Yes, of course."

"Bring Nikita to my office. We have to inform her and get her moving right away on this."

The prime minister nodded but hesitated as if he wanted to offer an objection. The president quickly refused any further commentary, pointing toward the door.

"Go. Get her now." President Yeltsin wasn't going to waste time. He stood up from his chair and followed the prime minister to the door. As the PM reached for the handle, the president touched him on the shoulder and indicated for him to stop.

"Wait a minute. Does Pavel Grachev know about this?" Yeltsin was referring to his close friend and the Defense Minister of the Russian Federation. Yeltsin trusted him most likely more than anyone else in his circle.

"It is possible, but I don't know for certain, Mr. President." The PM responded.

President Yeltsin gave a head nod with pursed lips and motioned toward the door, giving the PM the go-ahead to leave. As the PM quickly exited the room, the president traced his mouth with his index finger and pondered the consequences of two supernatural psychic spies, one loyal to Russia and the other a soldier with a pledge of allegiance to the United States of America. If Seth Phoenix were Nikita's match, it would be treacherous to all Russian secrets. Like a knife slicing through the veins of the Kremlin, Seth Phoenix was now their worst enemy.

CHAPTER 13

Nikita Oleshin's footsteps echoed as she briskly walked the shiny, pristine floors of the Kremlin. She stared straight ahead, only moving her eyes when she turned a corner as she was guided to the president's office by Russian Intelligence Director, Dominik Maslov. It was here in the president's office that she would be briefed on her next assignment.

Nikita was Russia's most-guarded military intelligence asset. And she was gifted. She was a Seth Phoenix match in every sense of the word. If there was a thought floating through Seth's brain eight thousand miles away, she could catch it in thin air before it had time to leave his subconscious. She was that good. Born with the ability. Trained and tested by dozens of scientists and medical professionals in the Russian community. The best of the best.

She had the unfathomable ability to move objects with her mind. Like Seth Phoenix, she could influence living matter and was once known to stop an animal's heartbeat with extreme focus. Now she had an adversary across the globe who was her match and could penetrate her mind as she could penetrate his.

Yet neither of the two supremely gifted spies knew of the other until the incident at Fort Bragg, North Carolina, exposed her supernatural match.

The president stood and walked toward the door upon hearing Nikita's footsteps clicking against the floor. The Director for the Foreign Intelligence Service of the Russian Federation, SVR, stopped outside the president's door and knocked.

President Yeltsin gave them permission to enter the office and stood to the side of the double doors as Nikita walked in and greeted the president with a zealous handshake. The president's eyes quickly assessed Nikita's attire with appreciation. She wore a charcoal gray pantsuit with black patent heels and carried a matching handbag. Even with her two-and-a-half-inch heels, Nikita only stood 5'4" tall.

Her dark brown, shoulder-length hair was neatly styled in a French twist, and her sky-blue eyes were piercing, framed by coal-black lashes that accentuated her creamy skin and perfectly shaped oval face. She looked at least a decade younger than her actual age of thirty-seven, even though she had spent the last five years in an environment that was unfavorable to an anti-aging regimen. An environment dominated by high stress and demanding physical and mental capacities. A daily routine of psychic spying for the Russian government could cause mental exhaustion and almost incapacitate any healthy individual. It required deep meditation that demanded hours of focused mental preparation. If she needed to exercise her telekinetic abilities to move matter, she was almost certain to experience extreme physical discomfort. Nausea, sweating, and headaches were common occurrences during the psychic invasion of others. But it was a price she paid for loyalty to her country. She had once served in the Russian military and had pledged her allegiance to her country, determined to make good use of her powerful gifts.

She worked for the SVR, Russia's official foreign intelligence agency, located in Moscow. Appointed by the president, Director Dominik Maslov routinely reported to the president's office each week. The position demanded uncompromising loyalty to Boris Yeltsin. Some of their conversations were not even shared with other members of the Russian government. Under the president's leadership, the SVR could receive secret orders directly from the Russian president without any approval from the Federal Assembly. And this was one of those times when the utmost secrecy must be exercised. Nikita Oleshun was about to be assigned her most clandestine operation to date.

President Yeltsin motioned for Nikita to sit. Her senses were immediately heightened, and she began to feel the president's emotions. He was anxious. Word images began zipping in and out of her mind as she sat quietly in front of the president, waiting for him to address her.

"Nikita, are you feeling well today?"

Nikita stared at the president and hesitated before answering. "Yes, Mr. President. I feel well." Her hands were locked and resting in her lap.

"Mr. President, you didn't call me here to find out how I feel." Nikita treaded carefully but knew she needed to quickly confirm the overwhelming foreboding that enveloped her. Her neck and ears had already begun to glisten with beads of sweat as she processed the mental influx of information passing from the president's mind. With meteoric speed, the president's thoughts slammed across invisible channels into Nikita's consciousness.

The president leaned back in his chair. "The United States has a spy with your capabilities. We don't know how long they have had him. But we know he is there, and we know that he is as strong as you are."

Nikita's eyes were wide. "As strong as I am?"

"Or stronger." The president's tone was pessimistic.

Nikita's eyes flashed across the room to Director Maslov and back to the president. "What else?"

Director Maslov walked closer toward the desk and leaned against the edge. He was didactic and forthright. "One of our recruits witnessed his abilities during a recent attack on an American army base."

Nikita looked away. "Our recruit? You mean our agent? Where is he now?"

The president hesitated. "He's not exactly our agent, but he is providing us with Intel on this American soldier. I cannot tell you more than that. The Americans know that we were there. You have to penetrate this man's mind."

Nikita let out a sigh. The lines on her forehead deepened as she contemplated the severity of the situation.

"Time travel and OBEs will be next." She mumbled to herself.

"What?" President Yeltsin leaned forward.

"Time travel, Mr. President. I will have to travel, but I haven't done that in a long time. It requires an out-of-body experience, but it's necessary if we want to really know what the Americans are doing. What's his name?"

Maslov interjected. "Phoenix. Command Sergeant Major Seth Phoenix."

Nikita nodded. She stood and started for the door. "I'll get packed and return here in a couple of hours."

The men stood and shook Nikita's hand before escorting her to the door. Images of Seth raced through her mind. Connecting with him would be easy, but dangerous. It would be more dangerous than any other military operation she had ever known. And it was starting right now.

CHAPTER 14

Finley glanced over at Seth as the two of them lay side by side in the remote viewing lab. It wasn't a typical remote viewing session. This was something different. Finley McCall was about to be tested for mental telepathy skills. Seth had to go along with it, but he was amused more than anything else. He already knew that Finley couldn't read the mind of another person if they stood in front of him with cue cards in hand. He was innocent. In the wrong place at the wrong time. Finley's skills weren't supernatural, but they were super badass when it came to pulling the trigger of an M24.

Seth whispered to Finley. "Hey, do you know what I'm thinking?"

"Hell, no. Do you know what I'm thinking?" Finley asked in a very serious tone.

Seth laughed. "Yeah, I do. You sick bastard."

Finley chuckled. "I wanna get the hell out of here."

Seth motioned for Finley to be quiet. "Shhh. They're right around the corner. Gonna cut the lights in a second. The party's about to start."

Dressed in loose-fitting clothing, their bodies seemed to melt into the plushness of the reclining chairs where they lay. Both men were wired to monitor vital signs. A chest band was positioned around the thoracic region to monitor changes in breathing, while a finger monitor was placed on the index finger for monitoring pulse rate. Blood pressure measurements were recorded using an armband fastened securely to the upper left arm, and communication with the men was finally enabled via a Bluetooth-like device placed in their ears. Dr. O'Connor and the remote viewing monitors outside were able to speak directly to both men while they were under. If Finley exhibited any of the same abilities as Seth Phoenix, his vital signs would likely indicate changes inside his body during the experiment. The changes were expected to be similar to those observed in other remote viewers who had tested highly in extrasensory capabilities. While the doctor wasn't expecting the same type of extraordinary results as noted in Seth Phoenix, he was hopeful of gaining another viewer for the program. If Finley McCall had the gift of clairvoyance, they were about to find out.

Dr. O'Connor passed through the hall before flicking the lights off and shutting the doors to the lab. "We're testing in three, gentlemen. Three. Two. One."

The lab fell silent as the men's eyes scanned the entire room. The temperature in the room settled to a comfortable seventy degrees Fahrenheit, and the ceiling appeared to open to outer space as the men watched millions of stars floating above them. A faint humming sound could be heard mimicking the sounds of the universe. The sound was believed to be recordings of noises from outer space and to be effective in sending remote viewers into a trancelike state.

The room was completely devoid of light except for a soft, pulsating glow emanating from an array of three small, fabric-lined lanterns positioned near the front wall. The room was windowless and almost soundproof except for the door leading outside, and its walls were bare and painted in neutral shades. Without a doubt, the room immediately invited a sense of calm upon entry, designed to induce a meditative state.

The Army's remote viewers knew the rules before entering a session. Star Gate has already successfully trained and utilized four of the best remote viewers in the country. Because the program was a clandestine operation, recruiting was difficult. When a new viewer entered the program, they came with a high recommendation and had already been scrubbed for authenticity before ever making it to Fort Meade. The program has only accepted one new viewer in the last five years.

A routine viewing session required learning to overcome any irritations that might hinder a meditative state. Viewers were required to assess themselves using a quick check sheet. They were asked to grade their level of anxiety and emotional state before entering the lab. They were expected to visit the restroom and advise the monitors if they felt hungry or thirsty. Any type of distraction could interfere with or prematurely end a remote viewing session.

The doctor kept quiet, allowing Seth and Finley to concentrate. Both men quickly slipped into a mutual state of relaxation, and the doctor hurried to begin testing them for telepathic abilities. But Seth was drifting deep. The doctor was losing Seth as he made a rapid descent within seconds, escaping into another world as he crossed dimensions. It was almost as if he had lost control as he found himself falling at the speed of light through a tunnel that looked like thousands of lightning bolts propelling him forward. He gasped, trying to catch his breath as he came to an abrupt stop in a pitch-black tube. Then, with the suddenness of flicking a switch, he found himself standing outside the front entrance to the Kremlin. He was fully aware of his surroundings and open to receiving information, but suddenly, he became vulnerable and was being watched by someone else who had crossed into this space with him.

A shadow was in the distance. It was nightfall, but the shadow moved forward without a body. Seth quickly crept to a side wall and attempted a telepathic connection. He wanted to invade the shadow's mental capacity, but the only thing he was able to decipher was static, much like radio interference.

Seth froze, not daring to make a sound. Even though it was clear that he was out of body and transported halfway around the world, he knew this other existence was reality. It was reality several hours into the future.

All at once, he sensed movement and human body heat encircling his space. The shadow hovered above him, watching and studying him as if it had reason to fear him. Seth jerked around and looked up. There she was suspended in free form. A woman with catlike, emerald eyes and lustrous dark brown hair. Her eyes locked with his as she penetrated his mind, forcing him to allow her inside. Seth grimaced as he felt a sharp pain in his head.

The energy exchange was explosive as Nikita Oleshun fought to gain control. The duo's energy fields collided, exposing top-secret information that each of them guarded equally. With locked eyes, they mentally analyzed the information as it rapidly passed through an invisible network. Within seconds, they knew exactly what the other had been summoned for. As top-secret information was being telepathically transferred, Nikita and Seth realized they were fighting the same battle. It was a global fight in desperate need of a unified war against evil infecting the very fabric of civilization. But could she be trusted? She was invading his mind, and he was invading hers. The two countries had been equally suspicious of one another forever, and now wasn't the time or place to question the shadow woman's agenda.

Seth Phoenix was seven hours ahead of Washington, D.C., as he watched Nikita's form hovering just a few feet from where he sat crouched in the dark. He had attempted to hide from someone who could find him even in his deepest recesses. She was like him. Not omniscient, but supernatural beyond most human comprehension.

Then, unexpectedly, with a sudden reversal of energy, Nikita's shoulders slumped. Her face softened, and she began to back away. Seth watched, unrelenting in his determination to push her backward using telekinetic force. It appeared to be working. Her own energy reserves were being violently disintegrated as Seth hammered telekinetic waves against her. He had to get out of there. He had to get back to the lab and back in his body.

Nikita was turning. She was backing off, but it was all a ploy. She had to let him think that he was winning before she slaughtered his energy field, wiping it out as she went straight for his heart. She paused and gathered her reserves. Then, with a supersonic surge of power, she twisted around and blasted Seth against his chest. He lifted into the air and flew backward thirty feet before dropping to the ground. He slammed hard into the dirt, causing a dry gust of sand to swirl around him.

The crushing sensation had knocked the breath out of him. Ripples of shock waves ran the length of his body, temporarily paralyzing him. He let out a growl as he rolled onto his left side. He coughed and spit as he struggled to regain normal breathing. If he had not surrounded himself with protective energy seconds earlier, she would have surely killed him.

Nikita saw that she had not disabled Seth Phoenix for long. She panicked and ran, desperate to get away from him. If he were able to compose himself and stand on his feet, she would be forced to fight him. She knew his power. Although she had managed to disable him momentarily, she wanted nothing more. She needed time to assess the information she had gathered. She had seen something horrible during their exchange of information, and she knew she had to disclose it to President Yeltsin. But what would he do with this knowledge? What would they do now that the United States was operating a secret spy program as equally sophisticated as Russia's? Nikita fell to her knees and melted into the grassy lawn. She fell fast and hard through dark tunnels filled with sporadic bolts of lightning until she reached consciousness inside the walls of the Kremlin. When she opened her eyes, she saw the president standing directly over her and heard him urgently calling her name.

CHAPTER 15

Seth gasped for air as he re-entered his body and gained full consciousness. Dr. O'Connor busted past the entry door to the lab and slapped his hand against the wall just inside the door, flicking on the overhead lights as he rushed to his side. Finley lay motionless, stunned and confused.

"Sergeant Major! The doctor shouted and placed his hands on Seth's shoulders, trying to rouse him, but he was already in a dissociative state that had transported him to another time and place.

"My God- I saw her. She was there." Seth stammered. A part of him was scared. For the first time ever, he felt a sense of fear for his life. And anger. He felt anger because he realized that everyone in his circle already knew about Russia's psychic spy. All of his life, he had believed that his gifts were meant to protect him, but now his own people were doing nothing more than using him as an experiment. And vital information that could mean the difference between being trapped in another world and maintaining a safety anchor here was being withheld from him.

Seth glared at the doctor. "You fucking knew, didn't you?" He jerked the monitoring wires from his body as he jumped to his feet. "You son-of-a-bitch, I almost got killed. That woman. Whoever the fuck she is--almost killed me."

Dr. O'Connor raised his hands and motioned for Seth to calm down. "Wait a minute. No one let you get 'anything' almost, Sergeant Major. I admit that I knew about Russia's program, but I didn't know who the hell-"

Seth violently shook his head and shouted, his voice bouncing off the walls. "I don't believe that! You're a lying piece of shit. She was waiting for me. And she's as powerful as I am, Doctor. Don't fucking tell me that you didn't know." Seth was now standing toe to toe with the doctor, looking down into the doctor's eyes, wide and moist with tears by the fear of what Seth Phoenix might decide to do.

Dr. O'Connor didn't dare move an inch. He stood frozen, not wanting to agitate the sergeant major any further, but what Seth said was true. He knew about the program, but the reality of Seth Phoenix's capabilities had almost surpassed his comprehension. He had invested more than two decades of his life into the study of neuroscience, but outside the walls of Star Gate, the theories that he believed possible were scoffed at by skeptics who labeled him as nothing more than a mad scientist fascinated with science fiction. The U.S. Army sheltered him from the naysayers, and he was well-respected within the Star Gate program, but let a United States Congress find out about what they had been running for the last few years, and all hell would break loose. The program's funding came from hidden sources that no one but the people on the inside needed to know about.

He needed Seth Phoenix to find out what Russia was up to. More than likely, they were just transporting information through their mole. They now knew that the U.S. had Seth Phoenix, but the doctor did not believe that Russia knew the full extent of his capabilities.

Unfortunately, the doctor's presumption was wrong because Nikita had recognized the full amplitude of his identity almost immediately. She recognized in him what she knew herself. It was an instantaneous knowing, and her meeting with Seth was all that was needed to unpeel the layers of his core. His supernatural abilities were now raw and out in the open for her to dissect. After all, she was his match.

The doctor started to back away from Seth, slowly putting one foot behind the other as he took a deep breath. He felt caught in a wedge. His loyalty to the United States was unquestionable, but he liked Seth Phoenix. Phoenix had been an unknown, just an average person living a seemingly normal life, until he became a victim of circumstances. Just a young sergeant major from Chattanooga, Tennessee, born and raised in Southern culture, Seth was just looking for a place to belong. That was the story that Seth Phoenix had divulged a few days ago, and the doctor believed him. The doctor looked down at the ground, then raised his head to meet the piercing blue eyes staring back at him.

"Sergeant Major Phoenix, I am all you have right now, and I know it's hard to believe, but I swear by God that I am on your side. You have to believe me." The doctor's tone was earnest and pleading.

Phoenix turned and looked at Finley, who still sat motionless as if he was glued to the chair. His eyes were wide open in disbelief as he silently wondered how the hell he managed to get involved in the current situation and, more importantly, how the hell he was going to get out.

Suddenly, Dr. O'Connor and Seth noticed the distress that Finley was under, and they realized that they probably needed to get him out of there. Beads of sweat glistened across his forehead, and his hands were noticeably trembling. Finley had no special skills except his willingness to escape, and the Army was wasting time by subjecting him to any more monitoring, but his loyalty to the program was now critical. He had seen too much. Would he maintain his loyalty to Seth Phoenix?

Dr. O'Connor sighed. Finley eased out of the chair and stood to the side of the two men. "What the fuck is going on?" He demanded.

Dr. O'Connor ignored his question and gave his final instructions instead. "Sergeant Major, you can go. It's evident that you are not a remote viewer, but there will be some documents that you have to sign when you leave. You were never here. Your family, your friends, and even your dog can never know that you saw the inside of this place. Do you understand?" Dr. O'Connor paused.

Finley nodded, then responded in a clear, loud voice. "Yes, sir. I understand." The doctor motioned with his hand, palm up, for the sergeant major to exit the room.

Finley stared at him for a split second. Whatever was going on, he didn't want to be a part of it. And neither did he want to know anything that could make him a target for the FBI or any other elite military operative. He was happy to get the hell out. He backed away and turned toward the door, not uttering a word as he lifted the handle. Freedom for him was the sound of the metal hinges creaking and the click of the latch springing into place as the door shut behind him.

Seth surveyed the doctor's demeanor. Dr. O'Connor's head was bent down. He studied his hands, picking at his fingernails as he began his confession.

"Sergeant Major Phoenix, we've known of Russia's spy program for a number of years, but the United States needs you right now and-"

Seth's face was twisted in anger. His brows were furrowed, his lips pursed, and his voice strong as he rebutted. "Cut the shit, doctor, and drop the formalities. I took an oath many years ago to protect my country, but you mother fuckers just drove me to the front of the fucking line in La-la Land."

The doctor felt a surge of guilt wash over him, leaving his face ashen for a moment. He nodded once and cleared his voice. "We've invested millions in this program. You know that we have a team of remote viewers. Damn good ones. They are the best at what they do, but when we found you, we realized that our so-called "science fiction" project was weeks away from becoming a mission we could now garner additional support for. We could get the extra money we needed to expand if we could prove beyond a doubt that remote viewing was real. You were the answer. You *are* the answer."

Seth stared at the doctor. Scenes flashed through his mind as he began piecing together fragments of past conversations. He heard clips of speech as it played through his mind like a recording. He saw the program's supporters. He saw their faces and heard their voices. Three U.S. presidents knew about Star Gate. Carter, Reagan, and now Clinton had all quietly supported the research, but they knew about Russia, and that's why they funneled over twenty million dollars into the program. The project had been running for decades.

Seth Phoenix had felt like an outcast, a freak for his entire life. He had hidden his supernatural gifts unknowing that the curse he so vehemently despised would ultimately make him a hero. He sat quietly, not wanting to speak. He only wanted to observe. His thoughts turned inward. How could he have missed this? Why wasn't he putting everything together? He was being unnecessarily hard on himself as he began piecing the puzzle together, but his focus had been on preventing terrorism. *Wasn't this the same thing? Russia's mission wasn't so different than our own. Didn't we all want to stop global terrorism using any resources that we had?* Seth leaned back in the chair and waited to hear more from Dr. O'Connor. He wanted to dissect every trace of information that was coming at him, whether verbal or telepathic. But before the doctor could speak, Seth motioned for him to wait. He held up his finger and pointed at the doctor.

"This time, you won't get anything past me. Nothing. I'll be in your fucking head twenty-four seven. If you expect me to be your guinea pig, you'd better keep me informed of anything I should know. Do you understand?" Seth's tone was commanding and left little doubt of his expectation.

"You have my word." The doctor nodded and looked him in the eye.

"I no longer think your word is worth shit, Doctor, but you and I have to play on the same team. You just make sure whose side you're on." Seth stood up and walked to the door. Hunger pains sliced through his body. His energy was depleted, and he felt weak as he put one foot in front of the other, headed for the kitchen. The doctor opened his mouth, about to speak and give Seth his next set of instructions, but before he could utter a sound, Seth answered.

"I know what you want. I'll be back here in an hour."

Meanwhile, thousands of miles away, the Russian president stood over Nikita. He laid his hands against her shoulder and gently nudged her while calling out to her. Her eyes slowly opened as she heard him calling her name. Her head felt bruised and ached as she rolled it from side to side, trying to get comfortable.

"Nikita, we heard you. You were talking out loud this time. We know what you saw."

Nikita's eyes flew open, and she stared at the two men standing over her. She leaned forward and spoke softly. "You know about the American?"

The two men glanced up at each other, then back at her. President Yeltsin nodded. "Yes."

Nikita breathed deeply. She rubbed her head and leaned back against the bench. "He's very strong." Her eyes studied the two men as she continued. "I wasn't expecting to meet him, but I collided with him before I could leave the Kremlin. It felt as if I was being conjured. President Yeltsin?"

Defense Minister Pavel Grachev now stood beside the president and rubbed his hands over his face as he studied Yeltsin's reaction. Grachev had been summoned to be by the president's side in the wake of what was transpiring around the globe. Grachev, a man of notable military skill, had once commanded parachute platoons, companies, and battalions during the 1970's, and Yeltsin had not hesitated to designate him as Defense Minister of the Russian Federation in 1992. He had a virile presence with his above-average height and large, stocky frame. And the scar to the left of his lower lip gave him an unforgettable look that accentuated his handsome, dark features.

"Yes, yes." President Yeltsin leaned forward, completely focused on Nikita.

"I saw a most horrifying image while I was fighting the American. I wounded him for a brief time. Just long enough for me to get back to my body."

"Go on. What kind of image?"

"Terror. It's terror of the worst kind. I saw a future event coming to America. It's coming soon. Thousands are going to die. And the attack will affect the entire world. Travel will be suspended. Total chaos will consume civilization as the attack sparks regulated attacks worldwide. This is going to be a global war, and it's coming if we don't stop them."

The two men looked at each other. Ice-cold chills trickled over the men's bodies as they processed what Nikita was saying. Do you know the details? The time and place?"

"Yes."

The president motioned for her to continue.

"The attack will happen in the U.S. at a major airport within the next few days. This is an Al Qaeda cell hidden in the U.S. They are communicating with other hidden cells throughout the globe and planning a simultaneous attack. We are a target, Mr. President. Thousands will die."

The president began to pace the floor. Grachev stood and walked to the side of the bench where Nikita was resting. His tone was penetrating.

"President Yeltsin, what direction shall we take? You must know-" The general stopped short of finishing his sentence and turned to make eye contact with the president. He waited for Yeltsin to respond, but he knew what they had to do. They absolutely must phone The White House. The secrecy of the two countries' mutual psychic spy programs had already been blown to hell and back. There were no longer any secrets about who was running a remote viewing operation. Now, the threat of terrorism demanded that a unified effort come together and position itself against a global Armageddon.

CHAPTER 16

The Russian leader did not tarry as he prepared to phone the U.S. He instructed the prime minister to get White House officials on the phone and brief them of his upcoming call to President Bill Clinton. If Nikita was right, the world had 24 hours to prepare for battle. And she hadn't been wrong in 99.2% of her previous predictions. This was an opportunity to change the future outcome of the present situation.

President Yeltsin leaned forward and placed his fingers on the phone in front of him. He hesitated for a brief second as he waited for the light to blink on the phone pad, indicating that the call was active and ready for him to pick up. Then the flash came, and he quickly placed the receiver to his ear. He heard the familiar sound of Clinton's voice. He had spoken to the U. S. president and Arkansas native on more than one occasion, and Yeltsin was always warmed by Clinton's candor and ability to charm, but this time their conversation would be brief and to the point. Clinton and Yeltsin shared an amicable commitment to share resources, even top-secret resources such as Seth Phoenix and Nikita Oleshun. Time was running out, and regardless of what the two countries' past had been, they now demanded unification, not separation.

As Yeltsin wrapped up the call, DM Pavel Grachev prepared to address members of Yeltsin's cabinet in another area of the Kremlin away from the president's office. After Yeltsin said his good-byes to the president of the United States, he placed the phone receiver back on the pad and made his way around his desk toward the door. He locked it behind him and began the walk down the corridor to the secret chambers of the Kremlin, where Grachev and other members of his staff waited for him.

As he neared the entrance, he could hear muffled voices and loud whispers coming from the room as the men discussed where their mission would take them and what it would entail. Nikita quietly observed from the front of the room, not needing to converse with anyone. Like Seth Phoenix, all she needed to do was "tune" into the chatter, and she could pick up multiple channels of information.

Yeltsin reached for the door handle, turned it, and pushed the door open. The room fell silent as everyone stood and acknowledged the president's entry. DM Pavel Grachev made eye contact with Yeltsin, and Yeltsin nodded, giving Grachev a non-verbal signal that the call to the United States had gone as planned. As the president pulled a chair away from the conference table surrounded by two dozen black leather chairs with members of his cabinet occupying them, he sat down, and all eyes shifted back to the defense minister. Grachev looked around the room, and in a stern, calm voice, he addressed the assembly.

"Gentlemen, you have all been briefed on the latest Intel indicating a global terrorist attack within the next 24 hours. President Yeltsin has phoned the United States. At this moment, the United Nations has committed to safeguarding our own countries and those of our allies. Our military units across all borders are preparing a massive force to face a global attack." Grachev hesitated before stressing every single word that followed.

"Gentlemen, we must, with absolute and unwavering discipline, adhere to covert communications outside the Kremlin walls. You are not to speak on any phone line unless it is a designated protected line. Do you understand?"

Some of the men stared back at Grachev and acknowledged with a unanimous nod, while others offered their verbal agreement. Grachev responded with a nod and a stern, hard expression, emphasizing his uncompromising stance. The reality of mass terrorism had left every single person in the room in somber thought and contemplation.

Meanwhile, over 5,600 miles away, Seth Phoenix strapped on the last of his gear, adding more than 40 pounds to his 200-pound frame. It was doubtful that he would actually fire his gun. Despite the Army's insistence that he be equipped, he had convinced himself he didn't need the weapons. He *was* the weapon.

The FBI had placed a ghost on the target, a secret spy who blended into society, someone who would rarely be suspected of working for the government. But their mission was simple. Track the target, get inside the target's daily life, record everything, and stalk them as a lion stalks its prey before the kill, but do it so discreetly that they are completely unaware of the invasion. The FBI knew who the target was communicating with. They knew what he and the hidden terrorist cell were planning in the United States, but before they could arrest him, he had already loaded all his belongings into the trunk of a sedan and escaped. He left nothing behind except scattered breadcrumbs and dried coffee grounds that covered the kitchen floor of an abandoned apartment. He was a member of the same terrorist cell operating out of the house where Seth Phoenix and the Special Forces team had raided just days before.

The sergeant major picked up his government-issued M24 rifle and headed toward the door. He glanced around the room with a strong premonition that this would be the last time that he saw the inside of the secret bunker known as The Star Gate Headquarters at Fort Meade, Maryland. He reached for the door handle and opened the door. As he stepped into the hallway, he saw the silhouette of someone passing into another room. He paused. No one was supposed to be in the lab. It had been locked after the previous day's viewing session when he encountered Nikita Oleshun. Seth stood rigid, focused on the lab's entryway. Someone was standing behind the door. Seth could hear the crinkling of paper as someone flipped through the files supposedly under lock and key. He put one foot in front of the other and walked toward the room, his feet barely touching the floor as he glided forward with stealth precision. He stopped and stood against the wall. He cleared his mind and aimed his focus through the wall as he saw who had entered the lab. There he was, standing in front of the cabinets encased in a concrete block. He flipped open a folder labeled "Sergeant Major Seth Phoenix" and read fast, tracing a line with his finger as he zipped across the page. Seth's eyes were wide and his mouth slightly open as he processed his thoughts. *Why was someone interested in his file? Everyone within the Star Gate Headquarters knew of his existence, and yet someone was walking toward the copy machine with his file!* Only two other people had been in the lab and had access to the entryway. Seth's breathing became shallow as he attempted to remain almost invisible and undetectable outside the wall. Seth watched, through clairvoyant means, as the traitor quickly gathered any information Dr. O'Connor had recorded about the sergeant major's supernatural abilities. He placed several pages in the copier's feed and pushed the button as the pages zipped through the scanner and pushed the printed pages into the outtake bins. Seth's mind was racing.

There was no time left to deal with this shit now. And who the hell would believe a psychic spy? That would be another can of worms to contend with. A psychic spy as the only witness who saw everything using telepathic means. The courtroom would be a damn circus. But Seth knew that the traitor intended to share the information for a hefty price. If he could supply Russia with any information that might aid their research, he would be compensated with more than 61,765,000 Russian Rubles, which, when converted to U.S. currency, would be more than 1 million dollars. He had placed a price on his own life, and if his plan was thwarted, he would stand trial for treason.

Seth backed away from the wall and walked steadily to the nearest exit. He absolutely couldn't let the traitor know that he had witnessed his willingness to commit treason. It had to be done differently. He had to disclose the mole's identity at a different time and place, with witnesses present. Although he was disgusted and overwhelmed by the burden of knowing who the mole was, he had to pretend not to know. Russia's spy had once been a loyal and dedicated soldier for the United States of America, and now Seth Phoenix's burden was twofold as he realized his responsibility. In less than three hours, he would foil a terrorist attack that would ultimately save millions of lives worldwide, and he would be the catalyst who exposed a traitor operating from the inside of the Pentagon and the United States Army.

CHAPTER 17

At least six dozen of the FBI's SWAT team positioned themselves in strategic locations of the airport campus. Seth Phoenix was positioned closest to the airport entrance and well hidden from any possibility of discovery by the enemy or an innocent passerby. He was well loaded for the mission that he knew was about to come full circle. His blood seemed to percolate within his veins as he blocked out any outside noise. His senses were all tuned to another frequency that only he could tune into. He had turned himself into a weapon of mass salvation in order to rescue a civilization from a terrorist who had become a human weapon of mass destruction. A human weapon that would be used in the form of car bombs and suicide bombers, determined to kill thousands of people.

A line of cars had entered through the front gates. They had passed the security checkpoints. These killers were masquerading as American citizens. It was necessary in order to carry out their mission. They had to escape detection, and the only way to do that was to blend in so that no one suspected anything. The element of surprise was their advantage. The element of vigilance and preparation had to be the American advantage, and yet most Americans were oblivious to anything beyond their own daily world of a hectic, rushed lifestyle.

A food truck went undetected as it passed through the terminal access roads leading to the back entrance of the airport, while a sedan had already parked in the short stay parking garage, waiting for the signal to advance to the terminal unloading dock. Both were loaded with explosives, ready to destroy entire sections of the airport facility. The truck was intended to target the runway area and disable all incoming and outgoing flights after a mass explosion that would take out a row of aircraft and anyone in the path of the explosion.

Seth Phoenix began to hear the chatter of an Arabic dialect. Bits and pieces of conversation stood out as he hastily translated the incoming words.

Delta gates. Runway. Ground level.

Seth grabbed the side of his radio and clicked the button hard and fast. He radioed the commander of the FBI unit, the urgency in his voice prevalent. He would give the signal that the enemy was now within his sight. Sergeant Major Seth Phoenix would cause the enemy physical debilitation as the FBI forces moved in to secure the area.

"Eagle 1, come in." The radio was clear with little interference. Only a crackle could be heard after the transmission.

"Eagle 1, go ahead."

"The Phoenix is Rising."

"Roger that. The Eagle will soar."

Seth concentrated, closing his eyes and allowing himself to see beyond what his physical eyes could. He saw the truck and quickly moved toward it near the rear of the airport's main terminal. He stayed focused on the driver, watching his movements. Seth took long, deep breaths as he prepared himself to deliver a crippling telekinetic impact. He rushed to the side of a wall and hid behind a steel pillar. He watched as the driver exited the vehicle, taking one last puff on the butt of a Marlboro. He didn't look Middle Eastern as Seth expected. *No, these terrorists were recruits. Homegrown motherfuckers.* The driver carried the square box remote in his hand that would be used to detonate the bomb. He glanced around the area before breaking into a slow jog away from the truck.

Phoenix rushed out of his hiding place and faced the terrorist as he ran straight toward him. Their eyes met as Seth raised his gun, taking a deadly aim at the eyes of evil. His stare seemed to penetrate through his body. Seth read his thoughts. He saw the gruesome bodies of hundreds of people that the terrorist had an aim for. He saw bloody lakes surrounding the airport, and he realized that the terrorist had already envisioned the aftermath of destruction from a worldwide attack. Seth felt a sickening feeling of nausea creeping into the pits of his stomach. He smelled the blood of innocent people, pungent and rancid. The sensation caused his mouth to salivate. He fought against the urge to vomit as he ordered the terrorist to halt. The terrorist let out a scream, shouting to a team of accomplices that no one expected to be there with him. They had been planted within the airport days before. Waiting until this moment. They rushed to his side, firing at the sergeant major. Shards of glass shot out from the nearby windows that were hit with stray bullets. Seth bolted away and dove toward the ground. As he rolled onto his back, he immediately lifted his arms in the air and began sending a titanic wave of telekinetic power. He then rolled away with lightning speed as he searched for cover, his ears ringing with the sound of metal mechanisms on their weapons breaking apart and falling in pieces as they clinked on the concrete ground. He heard loud, commanding shouts as the leader ordered the others to begin killing anyone within reach. They all chanted as loud as their voices could carry, creating an echo as they screeched and screamed the name, Allah.

Seth jumped to his feet and stepped out of hiding, into the open. The band of terrorists watched him while thinking that Seth was making himself a sacrifice. The lead terrorist dropped the square box remote during the commotion and now had the difficult task of finding it scattered somewhere on the ground, but he had to kill Seth Phoenix first. He contemplated how he would do it and whether or not he would take part of him as a trophy. He stepped out from the wall to face Seth Phoenix. His band accompanied him as they lined up to surround the sergeant major.

Seth Phoenix pushed hard on the button of his radio and called to Eagle 1. His tone carried through to every member of the FBI's SWAT team at that moment. And they all knew what he meant. His tone was haunting, and the effect would be everlasting as he spoke quickly into the mic.

"Eagle One, this is Sergeant Major Seth Phoenix of the United States Army. I am encircled. The Phoenix is Rising."

His words left a blanket of cold chills that fell upon the men hearing Seth Phoenix's voice. For those who did not know him, it was the sound of a man facing a fight until death. But for the commander and the rest of the SWAT unit who had seen the sergeant major's power, it was a Victory Battle Cry, a prophetic warning for the enemy.

The sergeant major extended his arms and lowered his head with his eyes locked straight forward. They glowed blue so bright they almost seemed iridescent, and his skin seemed to radiate rays of light that pulsed in every direction. His feet began to vibrate as waves of energy surrounded the terrorists who had locked him into a standoff.

In a frenzy of panic, the terrorist grabbed their backup weapons, pistols, and a few remaining AK-47s that had not disassembled from the telekinetic blast a few seconds before. They began pulling the trigger, unloading bullets that seemed to fly in every direction as Seth's tremendous magnetic force blocked them from their target. The lead terrorist flung his arms in the air, motioning to the band of jihadists with him. He screamed and shouted, ordering them to unleash all that they had as Seth Phoenix fought to maintain a steady stream of power that encircled him. He pushed with his hands, aiming the waves toward the men. The lines in his face deepened as he clenched his teeth. Within seconds, his body temperature soared to over 101 degrees Fahrenheit, causing his skin to become flushed and hot while beads of sweat trickled down his temples and across his cheeks.

The terrorists lifted their rifles and rammed another clip into the mag well. Split seconds seemed like hours as Seth Phoenix watched everything happening before him as if it were in slow motion. His backup was coming. The SWAT members were hauling ass from their hidden positions. Phoenix knew this, but he was determined to handle things on his own. He believed that his abilities would be all that was needed to end the fight right then and there, but even the slightest interference could cause him to lose concentration and weaken his stronghold against the terrorists. He needed the backup, and he needed it now.

The SWAT members moved in with the stealth precision of a lion, resembling natural-born hunters. Their footsteps were silent as each boot rolled onto the concrete, and their feet planted forward, moving fast and steady. Seth Phoenix could sense them coming up from behind. He felt the heat of their bodies and held his stance until he was certain that they were in position to take out the terrorists holding him hostage. If he moved, he might be riddled with bullets. He couldn't risk weakening the magnetic waveband that he had wrapped around the area. At this point, it was his shield and armor until he could gain enough momentum to start crushing eardrums and causing nose bleeds. Stopping a man's heart was not impossible, but the effects it had on his body were nothing short of starting a progressive debilitation. Ending another's life through telekinetic means would be the beginning of *his* inevitable ending.

The SWAT members seemed invisible as they maneuvered into position. Their motion was so swift that only a silhouette of their body was detectable as they moved to take out the band of terrorists. The team was fast and fierce but left hardly a moment for the Jihadis to utter a sound as bullets found their targets. The men looked like puppets whose strings had been severed as their limbs folded and their heads flopped to the side upon collapsing to the hard concrete ground. Seth quickly began to relinquish the wave of telekinetic energy pulsing toward the agents. Although he had weakened his force as the agents approached, he had not fully eliminated the vibrating rings until now. Seth began to feel weak; his body, within moments of collapsing, was affected by the extreme stress of telekinesis invading every cell of his body.

Suddenly, a scream pierced Seth Phoenix's ears as he looked into the eyes of the last jihad that now stood before him with his .45 caliber pistol aimed directly at Seth's head. The terrorist let out a guttural growl and stormed toward him. Seth felt a horrific crushing sensation envelop his body as he visualized and witnessed his own certain death. He dropped to his knees and struggled to maintain control of his power. The terrorist stopped short of pulling the trigger and jeered at Seth, laughing as he watched the sergeant major begin to jerk. He turned his head to the side and studied Seth. He waved his gun in the air as he suddenly felt triumphant and walked closer to Seth, who now leaned slightly forward. The terrorist stopped and looked down at Phoenix, his mouth in a tight, downward frown, and his pupils enlarged to the point of appearing like black prisms, leaving no trace of white. He sneered at Seth and spoke in what sounded like a disembodied voice.

"Sergeant Major, today you will die defending your pathetic ideas? Today, I will get to kill you. What do you have to say about that now, Sergeant Major Phoenix?" The terrorist pushed the barrel of the gun against the sergeant major's head.

At that moment, the sergeant major's mind came back into focus. He felt as if he was able to see two worlds at the same time. Two different realities, where one reality was refueling him with a power he had never known before. It was beyond his capacity and came directly from the Source. It was God's power. He felt his body re-energizing, leaving him with more fight in him, a fight to protect himself, his team, and the American people.

The terrorist spat at the sergeant major and slammed the barrel of the gun hard against the sergeant major's head. "Hey, answer me!"

Seth Phoenix tensed his entire body and stayed rigid as he took the blow without moving an inch, but he felt the laceration as the reticle on the barrel of the gun cut into his skin, slicing it open across his forehead. He slowly raised his head with blood now dripping from the tip of his nose. He looked into the eyes of the terrorist and suddenly jumped to his feet as he yelled with a passion that burst forth from the depths of his soul.

"Let freedom ring!" Seth's eyes were a radiant blue that startled the terrorist, prompting a quick retreat. He stepped back, but he wasn't quick enough as Seth lifted his hands in the air and projected the terrorist off his feet, now screaming and fumbling with his gun as he tried to pull the trigger.

Just then, an FBI SWAT agent faced him dead on. The agent pushed himself forward as pain hammered through his left knee cap. It had been shattered just moments before when he fell from a nearby ledge during the gunfire exchange that had severed his right earlobe. It now dripped blood and saturated the collar of his vest.

He reached for the blade in his pocket and yanked it out, aiming it for the terrorist's throat. The knife sliced through the air ten feet forward.

Swoosh.

It planted itself deep into the jihad's throat. The terrorist fell to his knees and slumped over as Seth released his binding force. A bloody shower began covering his trunk, and his eyes glossed over as he listened to the gurgling sounds of drowning in his own blood.

Seth jerked around and immediately scanned the area as he glanced in all directions. The scene was now quiet with nothing left except the dead bodies of radical jihadists lying scattered on the ground level of the world's busiest airport. Suddenly, Seth heard the radio static and the faint voice of Eagle 1 calling out to him from his position across the airport campus.

"Eagle 1 to Phoenix. Come in, Phoenix. Eagle 1 to Phoenix. Do you copy?" The commander's tone was urgent yet controlled.

Seth picked up the mic stand and placed it next to his mouth.

"Eagle 1, the party's over."

CHAPTER 18

Nikita Oleshun waited for a cue, but it never came. She was seven hours into the future and more than 5,000 miles from American soil, where one of the world's worst terrorist attempts had just been thwarted. The Kremlin was surrounded by air power and foot patrol standing watch. The best news that could be delivered was about to pass from the mouth of Defense Minister Grachev to one of the world's best-kept secrets, Nikita Oleshun.

She heard the twisting of the doorknob in the next room. Grachev entered and walked steadily across the floor toward the sealed room where Nikita had prepared to enter an alternative state in varying intervals. He pushed the heavy, wooden door open and met Nikita's eyes as he glanced forward upon entering the room. Grachev's expression was easy to read, and Nikita didn't need any further explanation, but she leaned forward anyway, despite her foreknowledge.

"You know?" Grachev took a seat beside her in a nearby chair intended for medical personnel who monitored her during meditative states.

Nikita offered a slight nod and slowly winked her eyes in confirmation. Her body's tension eased as she sat back in the chair facing the defense minister.

"And the Americans? Any casualties?" Nikita was apprehensive as she rubbed the prickled skin across her chapped lips.

Grachev shook his head. "None that we know of."

Grachev stood and looked at Nikita. Her face showed extreme fatigue. The skin beneath her lower lids sagged and was discolored in dark gray smudges. The whites of her eyes held remnants of exhaustion, with red zigzag lines spreading from side to side.

Grachev motioned for Nikita to leave. She was being dismissed. This war at this time was over. And Grachev knew there would be hell to pay if Russia's spy was now discovered by Seth Phoenix. The defense minister had been accused before of military corruption, but the mole inside the Star Gate program had assured him that this transfer of Phoenix's records would be clean and easy. He would simply make copies of Phoenix's files and transfer them by overnight carrier to Russia.

He waited for Nikita to meet him at the door and let her out first. The click of the door echoed in the empty room, and Grachev felt the finality of it as it slammed shut.

Hours later, after getting off the C12 that transported Seth Phoenix back to Fort Meade, the sergeant major took refuge at the Star Gate headquarters, where he showered and raided the kitchen refrigerator before being escorted to the White House. Even though he had sensed that he would never see the inside of

Star Gate Headquarters again, he was grateful to be inside its walls.

His head now had twenty stitches across the middle of his forehead from the blow that the terrorist had inflicted on him, but the Percocet given in the ER helped alleviate the pain. He was definitely a little groggy, but sleep would have to wait.

When he arrived at the back entrance of the White House, he exited the unmarked SUV and followed the Secret Service Agent to the West Wing Situation Room, where President Clinton and members of his cabinet waited. The SS Agent scanned his ID, then placed his face against the retina scanner. The light on the retina scan box flashed once as the door unlocked, allowing him to enter the highly classified, guarded room with over 5,500 square feet of meeting space, equipped with advanced communication systems and security measures.

Phoenix entered the room first and noticed General Monroe standing beside Dr. O'Connor and the CIA director, John Deutch. Monroe wore a regal look of victory. Seth's eyes locked with his as he stopped just inside the door. The general felt a twinge of nerves as he studied the sergeant major's face. An overwhelming "knowing" swept over him, and he realized at that moment that he was about to meet his fate. He began to fidget and contemplate a way out. Phoenix watched him, never breaking eye contact when he suddenly made a motion toward the door.

Phoenix stepped in front of the door and quickly slammed the locks into place using a telekinetic wave. He shouted with urgency.

"Stop the general! He's your mole!"

Members of President Clinton's staff rushed toward the president and shielded him, but Phoenix offered no threat. The threat stood before the president and his cabinet, masquerading in a military uniform he had once worn, loyal to a nation he had fought for. Now, the only allegiance that the Army general offered was in the form of his loyalty to money and some mistaken belief that treason would somehow benefit the world.

Dr. O'Connor shouted toward the general. "General, what the hell is going on here?"

The general froze and didn't dare move as Seth Phoenix stood prepared to blast him with a sonic impact that could crush his sternum. He didn't bother to look in the direction of the doctor as Dr. O'Connor rushed before him.

"General Monroe, you've been at the forefront of this program for the last five years. What the hell is the sergeant major saying?" The doctor's eyes searched the general's face for any indication of guilt.

The general stood stoically and refused to answer. The doctor turned to look at Phoenix, waiting for more explanation. Seth nodded in his direction as an affirmation that what they all were witnessing was the harsh truth, as raw and blistering as it felt, slamming into the depths of a patriot's soul. A traitor stood among them all in the same room with the commanding chief of America. The betrayal sent a wave of disgust among the men, and without warning, the doctor leaped toward the general in a hellish rage. CIA Director Deutch quickly moved aside, but his astonishment was obvious as he stood speechless and utterly blown away by the present accusation.

"You son of a bitch, I gave my life to you and this program. Star Gate. I sacrificed my family for this, and all you have to offer is treason? I should hang you myself, you Mother Fucker!" The tip of the doctor's nose touched the general's nose, and spittle landed on the general's face as the doctor spewed his wrath.

"I gave my life as well, Doctor. For the last ten fucking years, I dedicated my life to fighting for a program that was threatened to be shut down every other damn day. And now the fucking CIA is running the show. How long will it be before you find yourself looking for work, huh? Or will you end up on the front page of the fucking newspaper as the military's Dr. Frankenstein? And you have nothing against me. You can't prove anything." The general maintained a defiant post, but his tone was mocking and apathetic as he gestured with a slight shrug and flicker of his eyes.

A surge of heat enveloped the doctor as he clinched his fists tighter, sinking his fingernails into his palms until blood lesions began to surface. He stepped back as if he was going to retreat, and then with a violent force, he slammed his fist into the general's face. Monroe quickly caught himself and proceeded to engage the doctor. He grabbed the doctor's throat and attempted to push him against a wall, but instead, he crashed against the table, overturning chairs during the scuffle. Dr. O'Connor coughed and wildly swung his fists as Seth Phoenix quickly lifted his hand into the air. He blasted a wave of energy against the general, causing him to rise off his feet. His eyes grew big, and his mouth fell open as his defenseless body hung suspended five feet in the air before the sergeant major released him to fall on his knees.

Two Secret Service agents rushed forward and grabbed the general by his arm as President Clinton watched in stunned silence. They took control of Monroe and escorted him toward the door. Members of Clinton's cabinet struggled to regain their composure as they righted the overturned chairs and picked up the papers now scattered across the floor. Whispers began to fill the room as the men attempted to process what had just happened before their eyes. Within minutes, they witnessed a two-star major general, accused of treason, with the military's most powerful human weapon, deliver a display of supernatural strength that none of them were prepared to witness or capable of understanding.

Phoenix stepped out of the way as the general was led out of the room. All eyes suddenly locked on the sergeant major, and he heard the thoughts of all of them. Questions rather. Those thoughts were all questions, and those questions were about to be laid before a congressional committee over Star Gate. It would be a closed-door congressional committee meeting he wasn't invited to, and the most important question shaping the future of the entire program would be challenged. If human beings are capable of supernatural, telekinetic powers demonstrated by Seth Phoenix that cannot be controlled by conventional means, how can the United States protect itself against them?

After the general was taken into custody, the meeting quickly ended, and Dr. O'Connor was advised to take a couple of days off while the investigation got underway. Seth Phoenix was also given much-needed time off for a few days to recuperate and relax. But he was given strict instructions not to leave the country. Regardless of where Seth might decide to go, it wouldn't have mattered because the FBI had someone on him, always watching. From now on, Seth Phoenix would always have a ghost with him, that undercover FBI agent who blended so well into society that even the best detective in the world couldn't spot him.

The very next morning, President Bill Clinton walked through the door into a private conference area at the Pentagon. He nodded to the committee members already in the room, who were only a few top-ranking officials invited to sit in on the meeting. They all rose to greet the president as he entered the room. Clinton looked around the table, took a seat with the men following his lead, and then spoke in a determined tone.

"Gentlemen, we all know why we are here. Some of you were in the room yesterday when the sergeant major restrained General Monroe by supernatural means." The president cleared his voice and paused. His brows were raised as he glanced around the table.

Heads nodded. CIA Director John Mark Deutch shifted in his seat. He leaned forward and turned toward the president. "Mr. President, we have to have some way of measuring these abilities and proving whether or not remote viewing is a legitimate and trustworthy means of gathering intelligence. This is a dangerous operation that we cannot control."

"Star Gate has been in operation for almost two decades, Mr. Deutch. Two other presidents before me used it, but I am not disagreeing with you." President Clinton answered Deutsch but also glanced around the table, making eye contact with the other men as he spoke.

Deutch continued, determined to make his case. "Before yesterday, we thought we had a psychic spy who could time travel, but what I saw in that room changed everything that I thought I knew to this point. Nothing will ever be the same after seeing what I saw yesterday. And I don't know how we should address this. Should we continue funding the program? Russia has an equal to our Sergeant Major Phoenix. We need to shut this down. And shut it down now."

The Chief of Staff of the United States Army, Four-Star General Dennis Reimer, quickly retorted with fearless conviction, tapping hard on the table before addressing the members in a loud, commanding tone.

"You can't be serious? You want to shut down the program when we are just now on the threshold of an advancement that surpasses any technological advance we've made in the last decade? We made a discovery, Mr. President. Seth Phoenix is our defense. You must know this. I realize that the operation is not completely foolproof, but shutting this program down now would mean--"

Deutch quickly retorted. "General, with all due respect, Monroe sold classified documents to the Russians. They have the research on Phoenix, for God's sakes."

Steven Pomerantz, FBI Director of the Counterterrorism Division, now stood up and motioned toward the president with his palm up as he shook his head.

"That's a negative, Mr. Deutch. General Monroe never got the files to the carrier. They were found still in his briefcase."

Deutch laughed. "But we don't know what he shared verbally. Have you cleaned his residence?"

The president locked eyes with Reimer. "General, shutting this program down now is the only option we have. We have no weapon against a power we don't understand. This is a supernatural phenomenon that we are decades, if not centuries, away from harnessing. No one in this room is--"

"Send Sergeant Major Phoenix back to Star Gate for more testing," Reimer responded as if giving a direct order.

"We don't need more testing on Seth Phoenix, General." CIA Director Deutch spoke loudly.

Reimer glared at Deutch and argued. "Then prove that Seth Phoenix is a fake. Prove that Star Gate has no use to the United States Military. You prove that. Before you declassify any more covert military operations, you should subject this to unbiased testing. And don't bring any more of your damn hand-picked psycho analysts in here either."

Dead silence filled the room as everyone sat, stiff and paralyzed in contemplation. All eyes searched the eyes of another as the members considered the consequences of Star Gate and what its continuation would entail. The president pointed toward Deutch, motioning for his attention.

"Director, go ahead and get this investigation started. Arrange for a collection of findings within the Star Gate program. Get it done yesterday. The media is already chasing us like damn bloodhounds."

Deutch nodded and pushed his chair back, preparing to stand. "Yes, Mr. President."

"Gentlemen, if there's not anything else-

The president looked around the table. No one else offered any further commentary. The men stood, gathered their notes and jackets, and exited the room. As Deutch opened the door to leave, the president turned toward Reimer and extended his hand in an effort to stall his departure. He waited for Deutch to exit the room. Just as the door clicked shut, President Clinton stood and faced Reimer.

"We've got a hell of a mess, General. The media will be all over this if it gets out that we have a superhuman capable of telekinesis. This could start a global manhunt on American soil. I don't want this. This needs to remain a covert operation, no matter what. If I have to shut this down to maintain its secrecy, then by God, that's what we will have to do. Do you understand?"

The president's pale skin was now turning pink, indicative of the intensity behind his emotion.

Reimer read between the lines. "Of course, I understand. What the hell do you expect me to do with Phoenix?" Reimer studied the president.

"Reassign him. Make him disappear. You know how to do that. But keep him under your thumb. If Deutch's investigation doesn't produce scientific evidence of remote viewing capabilities, the Star Gate program will be shut down."

"Then why do you care about Seth Phoenix? If the Star Gate project has just been a waste, why are you determined to protect Phoenix?"

President Bill Clinton hesitated as he turned and started for the door. He placed his hands on the back of a chair and leaned forward, sinking his fingers into the leather. He took a breath and then addressed the general with his eyes deadlocked on him. He spoke in an uncompromising and firm tone.

"General Reimer, Deutch doesn't know what we know. He only saw Phoenix raise a man a few inches off the floor yesterday. Give Phoenix a new identity and keep him on our side."

The End...*for now.*

"People sleep peaceably in their beds at night only because rough men stand ready to do violence on their behalf."
– George Orwell

CHAPTER 19

A remote location somewhere near Fairbanks, Alaska, Sunday, November 12, 1995

As the chopper landed, the force of the Army Blackhawk helicopter blades scattered the snow across an open field surrounded by wilderness. Four Apache Attack helicopters flew in formation, surrounding the craft that transported America's soldiers and the most classified weapon in the world. As the Apache moved away and began circling the area, Sergeant Major Seth Phoenix shifted his 6'3" frame in his seat and stared out the side window of the aircraft. He was promised he wouldn't have to be here for long. Just a few weeks until any possibility of a media frenzy dies down. That would give the Clinton Administration and the CIA enough time to decide how to shut down Star Gate. Too many people were now aware of Seth Phoenix's existence, and four decades of paranormal studies were in danger of being exposed. Revealing the military's secret programs could lead to catastrophic vulnerability of the homeland.

Phoenix slowly placed one foot onto the ground, only to sink six inches deep into the frozen precipitation that now covered his feet up to his ankles. The wind blew a fine mist of icy snowflakes into his face, causing him to quickly squeeze his eyes shut. Two Army Rangers escorted him from the aircraft and motioned for Phoenix to follow them to a small, framed house less than 30 yards ahead.

The snow crunched loudly underneath the men's feet as they hurried to the front door. They stepped up and onto the porch. Phoenix stood aside as one of the rangers removed his right glove and pushed a ten-digit secret code into the lock securing the entrance. A small blue flash, followed by a single beep, signaled the men that the code had been accepted. The ranger pushed on the lock and opened the door.

Phoenix adjusted his military-issued sidearm, a Heckler and Koch .45, and glanced to the right and left of the ranger. He then followed him in and looked around at an empty room. The house was a shell with nothing inside to provide comfort. It was an illusion of constructed walls decorated from the outside in. The structure was designed to look like a little house in the woods, but it was a facade concealing an underground military shelter.

The two rangers moved quickly toward the center of the room. One of the men swept his foot across the floor, locating a hidden entry, while the other ranger quickly knelt and placed his palm and fingers flat against an invisible scanning pad. The ranger's identity was immediately recognized and recorded as a soft buzz sound. A low hum sounded as if a panel had opened in the floor, revealing a stairway and tunnel leading down to the secret bunker.

Phoenix knew the scene all too well, having spent weeks inside the bunker at Fort Meade. He started down the stairs. The two rangers followed close behind until they reached the door leading inside. Phoenix stepped up to the retina scan and leaned forward. The device hummed upon recognition, and the locks clicked open.

Phoenix turned and looked at the rangers, who gave him a thumbs-up, signaling the "okay" to enter, and at the same time, it was an indication that their part in Phoenix's transfer was ending. Phoenix nodded but hesitated for a moment before speaking.

"When will you be coming back for me?" Phoenix was comparing his notes to theirs and the time frame involved. He trusted no one.

Army Ranger Jason Garrett stared back at him. "Sergeant Major, weren't you briefed? We haven't received orders to return yet."

Phoenix studied Garrett's face. It had been at least three years since he had seen the man who had befriended him when the two of them were stationed at Fort Bragg. He had departed for Ranger training at Fort Benning, leaving Phoenix behind and uncertain of his role in the Army Special Forces division. That was then, but as Phoenix's piercing blue eyes stayed locked on his friend, he left no doubt in Garrett's mind that he wasn't trusting a damn soul.

The sergeant major nodded. "I was briefed." Then, without warning, Phoenix stepped forward and grabbed Garrett's arm. "I have no friends. Do you understand what I'm saying? I have no fucking friends right now. All I ask is that you don't let those bastards leave me here for months. I was told 'weeks'."

Garrett began shaking his head in exasperation. "We've got to go, Phoenix. The chopper is waiting. We've got to go." Phoenix read Garrett's eyes. He had been designated as the transport personnel but had wanted no part in the mission. He felt a twinge of regret.

Phoenix released his arm, and the ranger turned and ran toward the stairs leading to the outside. The chopper's blades, beating against the icy air, vibrated the metal banister as Garrett rushed to the top. He quickly climbed out and slammed the secret panel shut, locking it in place. Then he hurried to the door and across the snow, placing his feet back into the same set of footprints that he had just made minutes before. As he climbed into the chopper, he signaled the "all go" as the aircraft lifted off the ground.

Phoenix watched Garrett take his last step up the stairs leading to the outside. Then he turned and entered the door that led to an underground safe house. He was now in a 5,000-square-foot bunker with all the modern amenities he would need to survive. The underground pad was designed with a full kitchen, a laundry closet housing a dryer and a washing machine, a living room with a television, several bedrooms, dorm-like cubicles with bunk beds, and a full bathroom with a shower. The bunker also included at least five offices and conference facilities, as well as a small medical room stocked with a variety of first aid and surgical supplies.

Phoenix studied his surroundings and listened to the dead silence within the underground walls. He was now thousands of miles away from Washington, D. C., but was he as safe here as the doctor believed he would be? The United States government had been pushed into a corner. A corner that forced them to either preserve and protect Phoenix or kill him and erase any trace of his existence.

Phoenix walked into the living room and dropped his duffel bag to the floor. He eased down on the edge of the sofa and stared at the wall. As his eyes became fixed straight ahead, he began to feel a nauseating sensation and sharp, knife-like pains that radiated up the base of his neck and into his skull. He immediately recognized the pains that now served as a familiar reminder of the time when he was exposed to strong EMF waves. Exposure could cause severe sickness and interference with his supernatural abilities. He moved his head from side to side. He tried to shake the feeling and raked his fingers across the shaved remnants of his dark brown hair. But Phoenix had no idea that the bunker was located within a hundred miles of another secret military program headed by the U.S. Air Force and the U.S. Navy. And this secret program was much more sophisticated than the Star Gate operation at Fort Meade. Phoenix knew nothing about the electromagnetic fields that were pulsating dangerously close to his location. And he wasn't briefed on the proximity of his fiercest enemy either. Classified information had been withheld in a reckless attempt to control him. It had been two months since he had used clairvoyance. The last several weeks had been a welcome break from the energetic exhaustion that often followed his use of supernatural abilities, and he had not been given a reason to use them. Dr. O'Connor had convinced him that he would be protected, and Phoenix had believed him. Until now.

CHAPTER 20

Inside The Oval Office at The White House
Sunday, November 12, 1995
4:33 p.m.

President Bill Clinton greeted Dr. Nathaniel O'Connor and CIA Director John Deutch as the two men entered the Oval Office. Deutch closed the door behind him as the doctor walked to the front of the president's desk. In his hand, the director carried the final report and top-secret documents of the Star Gate project. The agency's final report included information deemed suitable for declassification. Twenty-plus years of highly classified research had been exposed beyond its perimeter. The special access program was operated in an underground world where fewer than 100 government officials were privy to its existence. Operated within the president's Black Budget, the CIA was now forced to shut down the operation or risk massive inquisitions from Congress and the public. Star Gate was the proof of psychic phenomena and remote viewing. If the research fell into the wrong hands, it could become the greatest threat to the country's security.

President Clinton stood up from his chair. Director John Mark Deutch locked eyes with the president as he handed him the declassified documents.

"The Star Gate headquarters has been relocated, Mr. President." The director waited as the Commander-in-Chief took the file.

"And Phoenix?" President Clinton flipped the file open and scanned the contents but didn't take the time to read anything in depth.

"Yes, he was transported early this morning to a classified location near Fairbanks."

"Fairbanks, Alaska?" The doctor's tone expressed surprise.

The director nodded and spoke to the doctor as he turned to look directly at him. "Yes, he was picked up at Eielson Air Force Base."

The doctor took a breath and studied the director's face. Deutch read his expression and knew that something wasn't settling well with him. He hesitated for a second, then spoke. "What is it?"

"I was just thinking--- The doctor rubbed his forehead with his fingers and paused.

"I was thinking about the proximity of Alaska to Russia. If the Russian girl---

The director looked confused as he interrupted. "We moved Phoenix to this location because it's extremely remote and only a handful of people know about it, but it's only about twenty miles from the base. If we need to get him out of there, we can do it faster than time travel, Doc."

The doctor nodded once and then asked. "Do you realize that this Russian woman can contact him if she chooses? She can penetrate his mind. See his location. The closer she is, the easier it will be. You just unlocked a door for her."

Director Deutch turned and looked at President Clinton. The president knew that he had to disclose further details about secret military programs unknown to the doctor. To protect America's most clandestine defensive weapon, known as Seth Phoenix, the doctor responsible for his health had to know about HAARP.

Deutch took a deep breath and motioned for the doctor to sit down in the chair next to him as he situated himself in front of the president's desk. The president took the director's invitation and returned to his seat as well.

"Dr. O'Connor, I need to make you aware---

Deutch took a breath and frowned, then continued. "About some information that has not been previously disclosed to you by me or anyone else at the CIA, as far as I know." The director paused.

The doctor looked at Deutch through squinted eyes. "Yes?" O'Connor's body stiffened as he traced his index finger across his upper lip.

"Two other branches of the military have been running a major research program for the last couple of years."

O'Connor's eyes widened as they locked in a near stare-down at the director. "What kind of research?"

Deutch shifted in his chair. "Similar research to the Star Gate program, but more focused on using and manipulating electromagnetic fields."

"I don't understand." The doctor cleared his throat.

"Doctor, the highly classified HAARP program is a research program jointly funded by both the United States Navy and Air Force. It's been summarized as a missile defense tool and a mind control device."

The doctor shook his head, indicating he needed more information. "Where is it?"

"It's located in Alaska near Phoenix's location." The director replied.

"Within 100 miles?" The doctor asked.

"Within 50 miles. And it's a very sophisticated system being used to test an electromagnetic pulse."

Dr. O'Connor wiped his hands across his forehead and down his face. He responded in a grave tone. "God damn it. I should have known about this before Phoenix was transported here."

The director leaned forward. "Why, Doctor?"

"These pulses act as a magnet with Phoenix's supernatural vibration. The electromagnetic pulses will consume him, depleting his powers. We've got to get him out of there right now." The doctor stood up.

"But we put him there because--- Deutch started to remind the Doctor of Security considerations, but he was interrupted by O'Connor's outburst.

"Jesus Christ, this could kill him!" The doctor shouted.

"John, wait a minute." The president raised his hand and motioned for Deutch to remain quiet. His tone was urgent and direct.

"Dr. O'Connor, we can get him moved, but I need to inform you about the significance of the research going on at HAARP. The program has been testing some of the same theories as the Star Gate program, but before we discovered the sergeant major, all of this was just lab work and hypothetical theories. We are at the forefront of mastering something beyond human comprehension, but we need to study Phoenix."

The doctor stared into the pale blue eyes of President Clinton, then searched his face as if he were expecting to uncover hidden messages.

The doctor felt his blood run cold. "Are you telling me that you transported Phoenix there to be studied?"

The president hesitated. "I'm telling you that the research being conducted within the walls of HAARP and the Stanford Institute is more sophisticated than anything you have done at Star Gate. And we have partners who are involved in stem cell research."

The doctor shook his head. "You mean cloning, don't you?"

The president looked at Deutch, then back at the doctor. "That's exactly what I mean. We need to study him, Dr. O'Connor. If Russia has the capabilities in Nikita Oleshun as we have in Phoenix, there's only one way to defend ourselves against them."

Chills crept over the doctor's body. "Duplicating his DNA?"

The president attempted to dissuade the doctor's concerns as he offered an explanation. "For the past three years, we've had more than a dozen scientists studying the phenomena that Seth Phoenix is able to generate at will."

A silent pause followed. The doctor covered his mouth with his hands and rested his chin in his palm. His eyes expressed doubt and certain fear at the thought of duplicating Phoenix's codes. Replicating them into an army of mindless human clones was the stuff horror movies were made of, and now the impossible was being considered in our race to stay ahead of advancements in Russian defense systems.

The doctor tapped his foot on the floor as he considered a response, but just as he opened his mouth, the director leaned forward like a lion cornering its prey. In a low and deep resounding tone, he confirmed the White House's intent. "We need his codes."

CHAPTER 21

Back at the secret bunker near Fairbanks, Alaska

The sergeant major massaged his temples and attempted to block out the interference that kept sweeping into his energy fields. He knew something wasn't right from the minute he exited the chopper. His skin began to tingle, and his stomach churned just as his feet hit the floor of the bunker. This was Alaska, and too close to Nikita Oleshun. *Didn't they know that?* Didn't they know that placing him on the cusp of Russia's front door would be the same as enabling Moscow's psychic spy with a telescopic sight that could probe Seth Phoenix any way she desired? The two of them had already proven that time and distance weren't barriers when tapping into their clairvoyant abilities but placing a top-secret psychic weapon along a back-door border just gave Russia an open channel.

Phoenix began to explore the other rooms in the bunker, finally making his way to a locked door that held secret answers to his sudden illness. He stopped outside the office and focused on the room inside. He felt weak and stumbled as he used his mental powers to enter the other side. If he attempted telekinesis to unlock the door, it could set off a hidden alarm.

Phoenix walked up close to the door and placed his hand on the doorknob. By touching the handle, he could tap into the energy of everyone who had entered the room and thereby access the information they held in their subconscious minds. His mind's eye showed him a cabinet with more locks, but he was able to penetrate the metal shell enclosing classified documents on a project he had never heard of. The front of a file folder was labeled HAARP.

Phoenix kept his eyes closed with his right index finger on his right temple and his left hand touching the door handle. Information flooded Seth's mind in a band of electrical waves. He struggled to mentally record important data as it raced across a railway of neurological connections. High Frequency Active Auroral Research Program. United States Navy and United States Air Force. Human Cloning. Mind Control. University of Alaska and the Defense Advanced Research Projects Agency. (DARPA)

Phoenix took a deep breath as he continued to mentally watch a mirage of research on a mental projector. He was stunned by the findings and unable to move, mesmerized by the discovery and the reality of the military's paranormal research programs. Star Gate was just the beginning, and in reality, it was hardly the central point of the research but rather an extension of an operation that was extending its roots into all branches of the military.

Phoenix hurriedly absorbed the data, but he took extra care to store bits of information related to paranormal remote-viewing studies. He made a mental effort to compartmentalize crucial data that might influence the government's interest in him. And as the pages of classified files flipped wildly in the recesses of his mind, the sergeant major stopped at once when his eyes met the secret files on human cloning.

Phoenix took time to read the first two papers in the file, making a mental note of the date printed in the top-right corner of page 1. *Were these the original documents printed and stored in this secret bunker deep in the Alaskan wilderness? And why?* Phoenix concluded that the documents he was reviewing were duplicates. These were duplicates of the original papers, bearing the wet signatures of the signatories. Papers that were now buried deep beneath the earth's surface.

Phoenix stood still, suspended in space and time as his fingers touched the projected image before him. November 5, 1995. That was just seven days ago. Phoenix scanned the paper and began reading aloud.

"University of Massachusetts scientists have successfully created a human clone using human cells implanted into a cow's ovum that had the genetic material removed. The human cells fused with the ovum and began dividing. Scientists (named in the official report) abandoned the project and destroyed the zygote when it reached the 32-cell stage. It is our educated hypothesis that the clone would develop into an identical twin of the human being whose retrieved cells were used in this experiment."

Phoenix sighed heavily and closed his eyes. A chill swept over him as he began mentally detaching himself from the viewing. He knew what was going on. He now knew why it was imperative that Star Gate be shut down and all traces of the program's existence be erased. And he knew the most significant reason for President Clinton's unrelenting need to protect him. He was about to become the government's most covert program ever. With the official operation now closed and the media silenced, the work could begin.

The sergeant backed away from the door and started to turn just as a surge of stabbing pain slammed against his face. As he fell backward, he flung his arms to the side and steadied himself against an invisible force that he wasn't prepared for. In the distance, HAARP was releasing electromagnetic pulses that had passed through the underground bunker's barriers and reached the sergeant. A normal person would most likely not be affected by the minute vibrations, but Phoenix was no average human being, and even the slightest change in electromagnetic fields could influence his tolerance of the unseen force and weaken his powers.

He felt a wave of pain and heard the vibrating hum as it pulsated in ripples before evaporating. His throat burned, and he began to cough and gag. His wrenching quickly caused him to vomit traces of bile from an otherwise empty stomach. As he bent over and grabbed his abdomen, he felt the warm, wet droplets of blood dripping into his hand. He examined his fingers and wiped his nose. As he touched the source of the blood's flow, his fingers became stained a bright, crimson red.

Phoenix was in trouble, and he was weakening fast. His supernatural powers became agitated as he now heard unknown voices. The sound of a woman's faint whisper repeated over and over. "Do not be afraid."

He slowly raised his head and began to put one foot in front of the other as he walked toward one of the nearby sleeping quarters. But just as he advanced a few feet into the hallway, he stopped dead still upon seeing the full body apparition of a woman he had seen once before.

Nikita Oleshun stood before Seth Phoenix in her teleported state. Although she was transparent, he could still easily look into the brunette's striking blue eyes that were just like his own. He froze, not wanting to put her on the defensive in his weakened state. He was vulnerable and didn't know whether he was a match for her if he had to defend himself against her power. She wasted no time and began delivering a message to him, spoken in English but with an unmistakable Russian accent.

"You mustn't tell anyone that I've been here. Your government is planning to use you by replicating your DNA codes. You mustn't allow this to happen. I am your exact match and a product of the Russian government's paranormal research programs. I have been under the control of the KGB for the last ten years. If your country successfully replicates our DNA, it will lead to the complete and utter annihilation of humankind. Do you understand?"

Phoenix's eyes widened as he listened to the faint, feminine voice of his supernatural mate. He stared at her in awe and disbelief. A distant childhood memory flashed through his mind, seeping in to comfort him and remind him of a time when he was safe.

Nikita Oleshun's voice began to trail away as the sergeant major's eyelids became heavy. He struggled to keep them open as he watched her, standing just ten feet away from him, now slumped against the wall. Then a loud and irritating ring burst forth and ended the dialogue as Phoenix's phone rang with an urgency that no doubt matched the circumstances. Phoenix reached into his right pocket and jerked the phone loose. He pushed the receiving button.

"Phoenix." He answered the phone in a low, gruff tone.

As he heard a familiar voice now loud and frantic from the other end, he watched the teleported apparition of Nikita Oleshun disappear right before his eyes.

"Sergeant Major, are you there?! Sergeant Major?!"

CHAPTER 22

The sergeant major immediately recognized the voice of his closest ally. The doctor was the last known person whom Phoenix believed he could trust in a world of powerful political agendas. As the doctor shouted into the phone, Seth fought against the dazed consciousness that kept forcing his eyelids closed. Phoenix's nasal cavity continued to drip warm droplets of blood that formed a canal as it dripped onto his lips and down his chin.

He then whispered into the phone. His speech was slow and slurred. "I'm here. What the hell is---? Get me out of here."

"Sergeant major, there's been a mistake. They sent you there — I didn't know, but I'm getting you out of there now. A chopper---it's coming. What--What is your condition?" The doctor was frantic. His words were clipped.

Seth took a deep breath. His eyes rolled from left to right as he looked around the room. "I feel like hell. My nose is bleeding, Man. Tell me. What the fuck is this?"

"There is a testing station near you. Electromagnetic fields. It's affecting you. I—

Seth interrupted. "HAARP."

The phone was silent for a moment. Dr. O'Connor realized that Phoenix now knew about the military program that had been in operation for at least two years, while Star Gate had been secretly operating out of Fort Meade. He hesitated to comment, unsure how Phoenix would react or whether he believed the doctor had no prior knowledge of the operation.

Phoenix spoke through lips now painted with blood. With his powers weakened, he was only able to pick up fragments of information from the doctor's mind across thousands of miles, but he was able to determine that the doctor was not aware of the program. "You didn't know about HAARP."

"I did not." The doctor relaxed and lowered his head as he spoke on the phone.

"Where are they taking me?" Phoenix asked.

A loud buzz penetrated the men's ears as the doctor began to speak. Static filled the airwaves, not allowing an audible passage of the doctor's response, but Phoenix was able to make out the faint sounds of the doctor's voice. And the words hit Phoenix like a sonic blast as he realized he might never escape.

"Homey Airport."

Phoenix dropped his head and mouthed the words, "Area 51".

Back at the Pentagon, CIA Headquarters

Director John Deutch sat across from President Clinton and Dr. O'Connor, who now listened intently as the Secretary of Defense, William Perry, delivered the latest horrifying intel from Bosnia.

"Mr. President, the Serbs have kidnapped a number of American soldiers during the last twenty-four hours. The last word we had was that they were being held for execution along with hundreds of Muslims already captured."

The electricity in the room intensified as the men shifted in their seats. "Do you know their location and condition?" The president leaned forward.

"Air surveillance hasn't been reliable because of the hostility in the region, but the last ground intel we have indicates they're beat up like hell. Location is an abandoned school building near Srebrenica."

"How the hell did this happen?" Deutch mouthed under his breath.

"We believe the attack on American peacekeepers came at 0300 hours. They were completely caught off guard. It's not safe for a ground rescue mission. The Serbs are firing rockets and heavy artillery, repelling any attempt to enter the area."

Dr. O'Connor traced his lips with his fingers and turned to look at the president. He said one word. "Phoenix."

All eyes turned to the doctor as the Secretary of Defense, Perry, asked, "Where is he now?"

The doctor made eye contact with the secretary. "He's in Fairbanks awaiting transport to Homey."

The secretary leaned back in his chair and shook his head. "We need him. Get him back at Fort Meade and get him ready to go to Bosnia. The only way we're going to get in there to rescue our troops before those bastards behead them is by some supernatural force. And Phoenix is it."

The doctor and the CIA Director glanced back at President Clinton as they waited for his response. Dr. O'Connor spoke. "Mr. President?"

Clinton nodded, then held his finger up and pointed to Perry. "You instruct the military that Phoenix is to be protected at all costs. We cannot lose him. We've got too much at stake." Clinton's tone was forceful and direct. Phoenix had become his own prized possession in the race to beat Russia's advances in military science. Although Phoenix and his abilities could never become public knowledge, he could pave the way for future warfare. A supernatural soldier designed by duplicating DNA.

The men started to push their chairs back from the table when the doctor halted them. His tone was urgent.

"Wait a minute. I just spoke with Phoenix a couple of hours ago. He knows about HAARP, and the electromagnetic pulses in the area are beating the hell out of him."

Clinton was silent for a moment before he turned his attention to the Secretary of Defense.

"Secretary Perry, forget about taking him to Homey. Dr. O'Connor will meet Phoenix at Fort Meade." The president turned to the doctor.

"Doctor, I need you there when that chopper lands."

"Time is running out. He needs to be ready to go in 24 hours." Secretary Perry added. The urgency in his tone was evident.

The doctor nodded. "Yes, Mr. President, of course." He pushed his chair back and turned to leave the room. He opened the door and walked out. As it closed behind him, Deutch leaned over and whispered to the Defense Secretary.

"Does he know about the research at Stanford?"

Perry shrugged his shoulders. "I'm unaware if he does or not, but when the mission is complete, he'll know. And Phoenix *will* cooperate."

"And if he doesn't?" Deutch questioned.

The president stood silent along with Perry. Both men hesitated to answer the question that both of them already knew the answer to. If Phoenix refused orders from the United States Pentagon, he could find himself walking into a landmine of his own making.

CHAPTER 23

Hours later, near Srebrenica, Bosnia

The chopper's blinking red and white taillights were barely visible against a cloudy night sky as an Army ranger prepared to assist Phoenix out of the chopper. The sergeant major positioned himself for the fast-roping maneuver and grabbed onto the rope as he swung himself outward while securing his feet. He moved swiftly and used his gloved hands to steady himself on the rope as he lowered his body. His movement was lightning-fast, like a fireman sliding down a pole, while heat-resistant gloves shielded his hands from the burning sting of the descent. In less than fifteen seconds, Phoenix was on the ground.

His feet were almost silent as they tapped the thick grassy earth. His stealth and agile movement were much like a lion's prowess as the sergeant major now found himself in the same mountain territory where American soldiers had just been captured and taken hostage hours before. Time was not an ally, and Phoenix knew that his assault had to be swift and paralyzing lest he lose the lives that he came to save.

A team of deadly special forces joined him as they exited their hidden posts shielded under a canopy of trees. Several members of the unit were American allies from the U.N., but the peacekeepers had not been successful in driving the Serbs out of the area as the invasion reached critical proportions. Mass graves were scattered across the landscape, housing the innocent bodies of thousands of men and boys who had died just weeks before from genocide or execution.

Phoenix looked into the masked faces of his team as the men huddled together. He quickly delivered instructions and then motioned for the men to move out. The team would have to provide a secure outside parameter as the hostages were being freed and guided through the main street toward the armored vehicles that would be waiting. Phoenix would be on his own once he was inside the walls of the abandoned town, now densely populated with starving citizens.

Phoenix wasted no time in his departure as he rushed down the hillside leading to the edge of the town. The building that reportedly held the hostages was located just yards from his entry point at the bottom of a deep slope. Phoenix's boots seemed to lift off the ground as he moved with precision. As he neared the outermost wall, he detected conversation coming from the other side. He squatted to the ground, then quickly found cover behind a thick band of trees where he sat down and waited a few moments. He homed in on the chatter coming from the hostage point. *Changing guards.*

Phoenix slowly peeked from behind the tree and focused his eyes straight ahead. Through the thick brush, he could see the town's lights and the statues of people walking in and out of the building that he was about to storm. He cleared his mind of all other interference until he was almost in a trance-like state. He watched and assessed the movements of the Serbs before him. Even the sounds of the creatures of the night faded as if they had never existed as the sergeant major prepared for the danger before him. Then he stepped from behind the trees, his eyes fixed on the target straight ahead. With stealth and precision, he made his final descent down the hillside and into enemy territory.

As Sergeant Major Seth Phoenix approached, the danger and complexity of the mission intensified as several Serbs began pacing in front of the building. *Had someone tipped them off?* Phoenix planted his feet firmly behind a cluster of shrubs, barely hidden from sight. He sent a magnetic blast to the Serbian soldiers that pierced their ears. Three Serbians fell screaming to their knees as blood poured out from busted eardrums.

Phoenix then ran for it, bolting forward. His blue eyes glowed against the dark night as he hurried past the fallen men. His body temperature was rising along with the intensity of his heart rate; He knew that the supernatural power he would need to access could cause fatigue and get him killed. But just as Phoenix turned the corner, he met more Serbs now responding to the screams of the fallen men.

Phoenix's finger rested on the trigger until that moment when hesitation was his biggest enemy. He fired off several rounds from the M4 strapped across his shoulder, the bullets pummeling into the thoracic cavities of three captors. Phoenix breathed fast and heavy as he dodged rounds that spewed from a dead man's gun. His lifeless fingers were lodged in the trigger pull of his weapon, and it had been his last and final attempt to kill the sergeant major.

Phoenix caught a split second of relief as he leaned against the outside wall. His eyes darted all around him, and his ears listened to the sounds of someone's whispers from inside the building. *English speaking. American soldiers.*

He heard the racing thumps of the Serbs' boots against the hard ground as dozens of them rushed from opposite sides of the building. Phoenix jerked his arms into the air with rocket speed, raising them with palms facing out as his body sent waves of electromagnetic energy toward the band of Serbs now determined to kill him. The mega-force of energy slammed into them, one by one, causing them to fall like dead flies. The popping sound of their ribs snapping like thin tree branches burned into Phoenix's ears as the sound of their screams followed the excruciating pain.

Phoenix maintained his position until he heard the radio signal from the outside team telling him to "launch", indicating that time was up, and he had to move now. As Phoenix's supernatural adrenaline flowed fast and hard through his veins, he orchestrated the top-secret rescue operation in split seconds. He felt an euphoric sensation as his feet seemed to lift off the ground, carrying him toward a blocked door that led into the hostage holding cell.

Phoenix raised his hand and slammed a bolt of energy against the barricade, sending it off its hinges. He then stormed through the splintered wood fragments and scanned the room with the agile skill known only to the best of the best in special ops training.

Wide eyes stared back at him in disbelief and horror as dozens of emaciated men and boys lay huddled together near the center of the room. The starving captives stumbled to their feet and scurried toward Phoenix, who motioned for them to exit the building. Fear covered their bearded faces, hiding the glimmer of hope that they had held onto for the past two weeks. As the last hostage passed out the door, the special ops team directed them to the caravan hidden by the night sky and waiting only yards away.

Phoenix looked perplexed as he viewed a now-empty room that was believed to hold American soldiers. *Where the hell were they?* He quickly adjusted his radio and clicked the button to speak but hesitated just as he heard mental chatter zooming into his mind. The pupils of Phoenix's eyes swelled as he began to receive visual information. Then an unexpected thud came hard against a makeshift door near the back wall beneath his feet. He sprinted across the floor and slid to the ground as he swept his hands across a wooden panel bolted to the floor. Mental images flashed before him as he visualized the interior of a manmade hole where the beaten and battered American Joes had been dumped.

The sergeant major breathed heavily before he spoke into the mic and notified the team that he needed help.

"Defender 1, this is Falcon. The nest is not empty." Phoenix's voice was clear, his words quick and clipped.

"Roger that, Falcon. Did you find Joe?"

"Affirmative, all of them are underground. Need assistance, over."

"Roger that. Stand by."

Phoenix then stood two feet away from the panel door and raised his hands with his palms facing down and directly in front of him as he prepared to send a blast of energy strong enough to crumble the metal locks. Sweat was now dripping from his eyebrows as Phoenix radiated a force aimed at the floor. The soldiers inside the hole covered their heads as they felt the loud boom vibrate the pit.

Phoenix reacted with a rapid fury as he bent down and wiped his hands across the locks, literally slinging the charred metal fragments across the room. He placed his fingers in a firm hold around the broken handle and pulled back with an unyielding force as he hurled the door into the air, sending it flying to the right of him and into the wall.

Just as Phoenix looked down into the pit, he sensed Special Ops Team Members, Defender One, and Raptor Three approaching from behind. He jerked around and made first contact as he signaled for them to join his location. With lightning speed, the men dropped their gear and lowered a rope into the pit as Raptor Three latched on and slid down into the hole. He spoke softly, giving the soldiers instructions as he assisted them in forming a human pyramid. As the men were thrust upward within arm's reach, Phoenix latched onto each one, raising each soldier out of the hole with astral force.

Seconds seemed like hours as Phoenix whispered the words, "Go, go, go!" Raptor Three zipped up the rope being held by Phoenix and Defender One. But just as the men turned to race out of the building, the terrifying, familiar sound filled their ears as they heard the repeated clink and thump of IED bombs being thrown through a window.

"Get out, get out now!" Phoenix yelled.

Defender One followed Raptor Three as the two men exited the entry point, and the rest of the team followed in retreat.

Time seemed to slow down as the sergeant major became disoriented. He had reached his body's peak energy expulsion and was about to lose consciousness as the last IED flew through the window, landing inches away from his feet. Phoenix shook his head and struggled to scramble toward the exit point. His body temperature was now dangerously high as he fought the urge to close his eyes. As his feet landed outside the front entry, Phoenix fell to one knee. A bomb detonated, releasing an ear-splitting boom, and the total desolation of the building's north wall crumbled before him. Shards of debris blasted Phoenix, slicing open his left brow as blood saturated the outer rim of his helmet. Then, without warning, he felt a swift and superhuman force grab him by the back of his jacket and lift him completely off his feet while dragging him away with a metaphysical speed only known by his own strength.

Phoenix's feet barely touched the grass as his rescuer raced away from the area, moving him up the hillside as he attempted to tune into the movements of Defender One and Raptor Three. He knew they had made it out of the building before the explosion, but it was no use. Just as he attempted to focus, he was dropped to the ground with a thud as the unknown hero, dressed in camouflage and now barely visible, stood over him, radio in hand. As Phoenix pried his eyes open, he stared in astonishment as he studied the figure standing before him, whose true identity remained unknown. The masked agent watched Phoenix and stepped away before offering an introduction.

The secret agent began peeling away the face gear that hid the agent's identity. As the mask was lifted away from the chin, Phoenix observed the faint outline of a smug smile followed by a voice he had heard before.

"Sergeant Major Phoenix, we meet again."

CHAPTER 24

Sergeant Major Seth Phoenix coughed and blinked multiple times as he stared into the pale blue eyes of the Russian spy. For the first time, he was viewing Nikita Oleshun in the present, standing before him, not a teleported hologram. That only meant that her strength had to be magnified thousands of times more than he had experienced months ago when the two of them had met at the Kremlin in an astral mission that threatened to kill him. And now he found himself vulnerable again to a supernatural human the world knew nothing about.

Phoenix studied her. Could she read his thoughts? Or was her power only limited to telekinesis? Before he had a chance to ponder the questions, she interrupted his mental dialogue.

"Yes, Sergeant Major—or can I just call you Phoenix?" Her Russian accent was heavy and her voice low, yet sultry.

Phoenix hesitated to answer and decided to remain silent for a moment longer as he continued to search the Russian's eyes. He was weak and not fully capable of delivering a massive telekinetic assault against her. Not one that he could win anyway, but his mental impulses were still useful in stealing information directly from the frontal lobe of another's brain before the words even had a chance of escaping their lips.

Nikita Oleshun was a dangerous, yet stunning beauty. Although her body was well covered by the armor and military attire that she wore, the image of her face carved an imprint in Phoenix's mind that would be difficult to forget. She had just saved his life and had become an ally at that moment when she lifted the 210-pound man off his feet and delivered him to safety. As he attempted to process the reality of the Russian's heroic act, he began to take mental snapshots of her features. Her piercing, almond-shaped blue eyes were defined by the perfect oval shape of her face. And her smooth, olive complexion complemented the dark brown twigs of hair that lay disheveled and strewn about her head.

"I should thank you for getting me out of there," Phoenix said as he leaned forward and started to stand. He decided to test the waters with friendly banter. It was worth the risk since she could read his thoughts anyway, and he could steal a moment longer until he decided what the hell he needed to do next.

Nikita nodded but didn't have time to waste. She then motioned for him to wait as she placed her hand out in front of her. "Before we move out—

Phoenix interrupted. "What do you want from me?"

Nikita took a breath. "My government will be looking for me in a few minutes. I have to radio in, or they'll come for me."

Phoenix's gaze became a hard stare as he zeroed in on her, invading her mind but wasting no more time and tossing the friendly maneuver out the window as he demanded answers.

"We can play this mind-reading shit another time, but right now, you need to tell me what the fuck is going on and why you just saved my ass."

Nikita ignored him and quickly jerked her face gear back in place. She motioned for Phoenix to follow as she sprinted forward, making her way deeper into the trees. The commotion from the IED blasts still lingered at the foot of the hill but was fast becoming a distant echo as she and Phoenix now moved out of the area with rapid speed. The night vision gear she wore aided in locating a cave where she had hidden out just moments before Phoenix's rescue mission commenced. She carefully stepped across a rocky path as Phoenix followed. He stumbled behind her but quickly gained his footing as the two entered the mouth of the cave. Just as Nikita made it safely out of sight, she rested against the inner wall and jerked the headgear off.

"My team thinks I'm dead. I have to report— Phoenix stated in a commanding tone. He breathed heavily and wiped his forehead.

"Listen to me. We have no more time." Nikita urged, her eyes darting all around as if she believed they were being followed.

"No, I have to- Phoenix argued.

"Just shut up. Shut up now! You can read minds, but you don't know when to shut up." Nikita blasted Phoenix through gritted teeth. The sergeant major stayed quiet, waiting for her to continue, and looking at her as if she had just lost her damn mind. He reached inside his pants pockets and pulled out a handful of high-protein rations. He quickly ripped open the wrappers and devoured them before emptying a canteen of water that Nikita handed him as he swallowed his last bite.

"I was sent here to gather information about you and obtain a sample of your DNA. We—I mean, the Russian government has been watching you since you were exposed weeks ago at the Kremlin. I am a servant to the KGB, now known as the SVR,

Foreign Intelligence Service. I am a prisoner of my government because of my abilities, but until you surfaced, I was the only known human of my kind. We believe that your government is also planning to use you. Do you understand?"

Phoenix began to sweat. Every cell in his body simultaneously seemed to come alive, and his skin began to tingle as dread swept over him. "Use me?" He knew what for, but he wanted Nikita to confirm his suspicions.

"Sergeant Major, Russia and America are at war to see who'll be first to replicate the DNA of a superhuman."

Phoenix rested his forearm against his head and wiped away particles of sand and dirt that stuck to his skin during the explosion. He sighed heavily as he spoke. "They're planning to engineer a damn supernatural army."

"That is correct. You were transported to Alaska for research. I've been in your head for weeks."

Phoenix frowned and glanced at Nikita with one eyebrow cocked. "But Alaska didn't work out as planned."

Nikita nodded. "HAARP. The U.S. Navy and Air Force have been partners in the program since 1993."

"Electromagnetic field testing for controlling the weather?" Phoenix inquired but knew the Russian probably already knew more than he did.

Nikita laughed, then replied in her heavy Russian accent, her words pronounced in a mocking tone. "Is that what they say?"

Phoenix huffed and forced a half-cocked smile, but he was feeling more overwhelmed by the second. "No, mind control."

"What now? We can't stay here." Phoenix's tone changed abruptly as he demanded to know Nikita Oleshun's next move.

"The Kremlin is tracking me. I have to report what happened back there."

"That mission was highly classified. No one knew about it." Phoenix stated. He instantly realized the magnitude of Nikita Oleshun's breach.

"As I said, I've been with you. When I realized what our governments were doing, I knew I could no longer remain loyal to the country that I loved and served for all these years. They have become something else. Something that threatens civilization as we know it."

Her voice trailed off at the end of her last sentence. At once, the Russian spy remembered a time from her past, an easier life ten years before, when she was in love and free from the constraints of her powers. As a sergeant in the Russian military, Nikita had become the country's most guarded and clandestine citizen.

Like Phoenix, Nikita's supernatural powers were discovered during a deadly battle that sent her directly into an artillery barrage. The attack happened ten years before, while Nikita and her fiancé were serving in Kabul. Because military romance was frowned upon, the two Russian soldiers had loved each other in secret. Their love had gone unknown until then, but they had high hopes of leaving the Russian army and starting a life together.

That fatal moment ensued as a blazing projectile of bullets filled the air, exploding dozens of metal cartridges in every direction as she fought to save Sergei's life. Nikita sent an electromagnetic force forward, crushing the assailant's heart as his sternum split in half from the impact. Blood spurted from his mouth as he fell to the ground, but it was too late for Sergei, who had taken a shot that severed his jugular.

Nikita Oleshun wailed as she stood over the body of the man who was to be her husband. Her knees buckled from under her, and she fell by his side as she lifted him into her arms. She kissed his eyelids and brushed her lips against his while mumbling "I love you" between gut-wrenching sobs. The horrific event was now a distant memory, but she still felt a sting of pain each time she remembered the warmth of his love and the emptiness she had felt without it for the past ten years.

Nikita shook herself back to reality and stared back into the eyes of a man whose physical traits resembled those of the man and the memory she cherished. There had been no one else who had come close to filling her heart since Sergei's death, and yet she inwardly begged to be relieved from his memory's grip. Lonely had become her middle name.

Phoenix's eyes blinked in response to Nikita's confession. At that moment, he felt one with her. He now knew her story and how the two of them had come to this place. It was as if destiny had led them here, and there was no other explanation for it. Phoenix had not known a woman's real love in years. Cursed by his own belief that no one would ever accept his strangeness, he had never married and had been alone for the past couple of years, other than the few meaningless, short-lived romances that he had entertained. It had ultimately left him unfulfilled and emptier than ever, but he had no remedy for his anguish. No solution or fix. And so, he maintained the familial relationships that had proven tried and true throughout his life back in Chattanooga. It was his safe place.

Now Nikita Oleshun stood before him, her soul naked and undone. At that moment, he realized that he had a friend and an equal but staying with her meant certain death to them both.

"I have to go." Phoenix forced the words out of his mouth.

Nikita stared into Phoenix's eyes, which appeared pained and soulful as he looked at her. She felt his vibration and knew that he would no longer be a threat to her. "Phoenix?"

The sergeant major sensed what she was about to ask. He placed his hand in hers, giving it a soft squeeze, and answered before the words left her lips. "I will."

Nikita then stated the secret landline numbers aloud.

"01174951230001."

Just then and without warning, Nikita's radio began to buzz. A voice broke through the static with an urgent call to the Russian spy now guilty of treason. She flinched and placed her finger on the receiver as Seth Phoenix turned and disappeared into the dark.

CHAPTER 25

The special ops commander, Defender One, repeatedly sought contact with Phoenix while shouting into the radio mic. The sergeant major could now hear the static of radio traffic as the commander's voice bled in and out in a maddening attempt to reach him, but Phoenix hesitated to answer. Although he knew he had to escape the area, he also realized that he had to think fast. He had just been rescued by Russia's coveted agent, and she was now in danger of being charged with a crime punishable by death if the Russians discovered her betrayal.

The soles of Phoenix's feet were hot, and his legs ached from the high speed of his retreat as he left Nikita Oleshun behind. He slowed his pace until he reached a stopping point near the site where the chopper had first dropped him. He bent over and rested his hands on his knees as he listened to fragments of noise up to a mile away. He breathed deep, relaxing his body from the sudden spike of energy he had managed to regain. The sound of the helicopter's blades chopped through the night air as Phoenix zeroed in and assessed the distance of the bird that would be landing within minutes.

Phoenix had to make a quick determination about the Russian soldier-turned-spy. If he failed to disclose his encounter with her, he could be arrested, but if the plot was as deep as she disclosed, his life and the future life of mankind might be at stake. Duplicating the DNA of Seth Phoenix and Nikita Oleshun could have cataclysmic consequences, but the two most powerful governments on the planet were now arranging plans to use both of the superhumans as lab specimens. He had to maintain a stance of ignorance for the moment. Just until he reaches the homeland. He had to return to Fort Meade in spite of the White House's determination to place him at Homey Airport.

Phoenix spotted the chopper's location as he continued north. He halted for a second and held his breath as he focused on the narrow path before him. The bird was there to pick him up, and he could no longer ignore the loud radio signals now coming through. He had to answer. How would he account for the loss of time since escaping the explosion? He would have to hope no one asked any questions. At this point, no one had any reason to be suspicious, but Phoenix simply could not divulge the details of what had just occurred with Nikita Oleshun.

Phoenix reached down and placed his finger on the receiver button. He applied a crushing force to the device, disabling it from sending communications. Nobody on the special ops team needed to know that she had even been there. He knew if he disclosed her identity or location to anyone, he would be risking her life and possibly his own. Although the government had promised the sergeant major uncompromising support and cover, he knew there was no one whom he could trust. Dr. Nathaniel O'Connor had pledged to safeguard the sergeant major, but

Phoenix knew that the doctor's efforts would be thwarted if the big shots at the CIA decided he was a threat.

Phoenix's mind reeled as he processed information and scenarios through his mind. He broke into a fast run as soon as he moved into a clearing where he was now visible to the men loading the chopper. Defender One immediately noticed the sergeant major and ran to meet him. He shouted, but his voice was muffled by the loud thunder of the chopper's blades.

Phoenix read the commander's lips and nodded as he rushed to the side opening. He quickly placed one foot on the landing and hoisted himself in as Defender One followed.

Phoenix buckled the seatbelt and leaned back, resting his head on the back of the seat. The crew that had just escaped the IED seconds before it detonated now sat before him with questioning eyes. The sergeant major refrained from engaging in any banter as he attempted to relax his body, but a sudden and unanticipated surge of information crossed his mind, causing a sense of dread.

As the chopper began to lift off the ground, Phoenix became anxious. He grabbed his seat buckle and yanked at the belt, slinging it to the side just as the crew chief and the co-pilot glanced over at Phoenix as he was moving out of his seat.

"Sergeant Major, what are you doing?" The crew chief motioned for Phoenix to stop.

Phoenix ignored him and moved closer, positioning himself behind the pilot's seat. "Major, where are you taking me?"

Phoenix knew before he answered. The pilot glanced around. "Don't you know?"

Phoenix remained quiet, his eyes locked on the crew chief sitting beside him.

"You'll be departing for home the same way that you arrived." The pilot confirmed.

At that moment, Phoenix realized that the messages he was picking up on were coming straight from the Pentagon. He was being rerouted to Homey Airport after landing at Fort Meade. The sergeant major calmed down and eased back into his seat. He had to get off that plane and contact the doctor. He felt a sigh of relief for a brief moment until he overheard a startling statement from the cockpit.

"We have orders to transport Phoenix to Homey after we reach the homeland. He is not to leave our command."

Phoenix jumped forward, returning to the same position behind the pilot's seat. He gave the crew chief a warning stare as the crew chief reached to unfasten his seatbelt. Then Phoenix spoke in a loud, indisputable tone.

"Sergeant, I don't give a fuck what your orders are or who the fuck they came from. I'm getting off that plane when it reaches Fort Meade."

CHAPTER 26

Back at The Pentagon

The sound of the doctor's footsteps echoed through the halls of The Pentagon as he walked briskly toward Director Deutch's office. He knew that Phoenix would be returning to Fort Meade. The commander had already radioed central command about the explosion before Phoenix ever made it to the chopper. The doctor knew about the final orders. Phoenix would be hidden underground at Area 51, under the control of the U.S. government and the world's highest level of military security. If someone wanted Phoenix dead or planned to kidnap him, it would be impossible.

The doctor reached Deutch's office and knocked on the door. He heard the director's voice as the door opened from the inside. As O'Connor entered the room, he scanned the faces of the men and wondered which ones were behind the DNA operation designed to duplicate Phoenix's codes. The doctor walked around the table and took a seat across from the director. The director immediately addressed the doctor as he sat down.

"Phoenix barely escaped alive." The director maintained a calm tone.

Dr. O'Connor's eyes widened. "What happened?"

"Central Command informed us that Phoenix was caught inside after the rest of the hostages cleared. Serbians then stormed the building with IED's. Phoenix miraculously made it out just as they detonated, but---

"He's en route here? I want to see him." The doctor interrupted."

"Yes, the plane will land here, but the crew has orders to immediately transport Phoenix to Homey."

The doctor shook his head. "I need to see him. You know that I've been at the forefront of this research and this program since the beginning. I need to evaluate his condition."

The director hesitated, then continued. "We don't think that's a good idea, doctor."

"What? What are you talking about?" The doctor never cared much for Deutch and considered him a sneaky bastard.

The director turned and looked at the president, then back at the doctor. "We think Phoenix was *rescued*." The director emphasized his last word.

"Rescued?"

"Yes, rescued. Phoenix was the last known person inside that building when it blew. And it was loaded to hell and back with explosives. The rest of the team watched the inferno from the trees. Phoenix was nowhere to be found. Until---

"What the hell are you saying? Why did you send Phoenix to Bosnia? The sergeant major doesn't need to be rescued. He's capable—

The director nodded and held up his index finger. "Yes, but intel informed us yesterday that Russia had deployed troops to

Srebrenica. We believe one of those soldiers was Nikita Oleshun."

The doctor slowly leaned forward. "What the hell is going on? Nikita Oleshun is-- "

Deutch interrupted, forcing the doctor to listen. "That is correct, Doctor. We now have intel that confirms Russia's DNA research. If the Russians succeed, they will be the first superpower capable of producing a soldier like their own Nikita Oleshun."

"My God. How long has this been going on?"

The director took a breath. "Years, maybe. But we believe Nikita Oleshun was in Srebrenica during this operation." The director tapped the table.

Dr. O'Connor traced his index finger across his lips as he considered the possibility that Oleshun had helped Phoenix escape. If she had helped the sergeant major or given him any information, she could have been charged with treason by the Russian government.

"We cannot pursue this research on Phoenix. We cannot be a part of something of this magnitude. This idea of duplicating Phoenix's DNA to reproduce superhuman soldiers. It's unethical. This soldier—the sergeant major---he's a man, not a damn robot."

No one spoke as the doctor continued. "Gentlemen, we've been cloning since 1952, when the first tadpole was cloned. But that doesn't make this research appropriate for humans. To hell with your agendas. To hell with the research. This is a treacherous attempt at world domination, and I'm going to tell you --- and."

The doctor paused and looked into the faces of the men now listening to him through narrowed eyes. Dr. O'Connor realized he was alone at that moment. He was stating an opposition that no one else in the room supported. As the doctor absorbed the coldness of their stares, he issued a final and fateful warning on the sergeant major's behalf.

"Phoenix will never agree to let you do this. He'll never agree to give you what you want. If you try to force the sergeant major into this, you'll be opening a Pandora's box. He has killed before, Gentlemen. We trained him to recognize the enemy. You'd better be certain that he doesn't mistake you for one."

Director Deutch shifted in his chair as the president turned to the doctor.

"What time is that plane due at Meade?" The president asked and looked back at Deutch.

The director was consumed with the reality of the consequences before him. After a long pause, he mumbled aloud and glanced in the doctor's direction. "Nine hours. He'll be there in nine hours."

CHAPTER 27

MOSCOW, The Kremlin

Nikita Oleshun adjusted her sidearm and unfastened the seatbelt strapped across her legs as the Russian Mil Mi-24 helicopter gunship, otherwise known as "Crocodile," landed outside the Kremlin. As she stood up and moved toward the side door, she felt a pair of powerful eyes watching her as she exited. She placed her hand on the side of the door and quickly searched the perimeter of people now gathering on the landing pad. Just as she scanned the rear left of the chopper, she locked eyes with Prime Minister Vladimir Putin, who maintained a poker face.

Nikita sensed impending danger and, without further hesitation, began accessing Putin's thoughts. She deliberately looked away from the prime minister and stepped out of the attack helicopter, placing one foot at a time on the side-step ladder leading to the ground. As Nikita sent invisible currents across the distance, penetrating Putin's mind, she caught herself just as she was about to gasp aloud. *He knew she was there.* Inside his mind. And he was playing it to his advantage, leading the

Russian spy into a Machiavellian territory she wasn't prepared for.

Putin sent a signal aimed at Nikita Oleshun. He intended for her to see the images that he was producing in his mind. Images of her participation in the Kremlin-backed research for human cloning. The Russians had already produced the first psychic spy in the world, and they would be the first to produce multiples of her offspring. Genetically engineered to lead the race to become the most powerful country on the planet.

Nikita's blood ran cold the moment she looked into his mind. Although Putin was intentionally juggling his thoughts like a recorder repeatedly rewinding its data, she was able to hear the prime minister's future conversation, and she managed to slice through the veil of deception. He was there to escort her directly to President Yeltsin, who was waiting along with members of the Foreign Intelligence Service. She was about to give her debriefing of the Americans' mission in Srebrenica. And the Kremlin already knew she had been there.

Nikita had to make a quick decision about how to assume an apathetic posture toward Phoenix. *Could she disguise herself from the government that had taught her the ways of being a spy?* She had to. She had no choice. If she exposed herself now, they would kill her. She was certain of it. She had to convince them that Phoenix was dead.

Putin spoke to Nikita and motioned for her to enter the SUV. As she stepped forward, the prime minister lightly brushed against her forearm. A surge of images flashed before her, sending her into a dizzy spin as she struggled to maintain her balance. Nikita quickly fought off the urge to vomit and climbed into the vehicle. As she sat down and leaned back against the seat, her lips moved in a silent affirmation. *There is no other way out now.*

Fort Meade, Maryland
Department of Homeland Security
1500 hours

The sound of Deutch's shoes on the pristine, polished floor of the Department of Homeland Security could be heard as he approached the classified area reserved for top-secret meetings. Phoenix was just seconds behind the unsuspecting director, pushing past anything and anyone in his way as he neared Hall C. Dr. O'Connor was inside waiting. The doctor was prepared for his arrival. He had a medical kit in hand and three lunch trays that he had ordered to be delivered as soon as he got word that the chopper had landed on the base. By the time the sergeant major arrived, the food would be ready and delivered from the campus cafeteria.

O'Connor knew how detrimental it was for Phoenix to be fully replenished after enduring an episode of telekinesis. The depletion of energy could take days to recover if he was not fully restored by nutrition and intravenous fluids. The supernatural gift came with a high-maintenance price.

Phoenix passed the retina scan and slammed his forearm against the door as he made a hard entry into the room. Deutch froze as he observed the sergeant major standing before him. Phoenix was dirty and greasy, his hair disheveled, and his hands covered with scrapes and scratches from the shards of debris that blasted forth from the explosion. His body ached now, and he needed food. Lots of it. Although he was gravely weakened, his present state served as a warning to the doctor who knew his

176

capabilities and the severity of consequences that could develop if Phoenix wasn't able to control his impulses.

"Sergeant Major." The doctor jumped to his feet as he spoke.

Phoenix stopped just inside the door.

The doctor motioned for Phoenix to sit. The sergeant major paused, searching the eyes of the men before collapsing into a rolling chair seated in front of the doctor. Phoenix stared at Dr. O'Connor through bloodshot eyes.

"Doc, get me-- Phoenix's speech became slurred as he was overcome with a need for sleep. He slumped forward and then, without warning, Phoenix jerked upright. The table began to vibrate, and the men stared in shock and awe.

The doctor wasted no time and quickly jumped around the table to Phoenix's side as he opened his medical bag and administered an injection of Valium. The injection immediately calmed his muscle reactions and slowed his heart rate and breathing. Because Phoenix couldn't control his bodily impulses during periods of severe depletion, it was imperative that he slow his metabolism and begin metabolic restoration. Although its effects on his central nervous system were short-lived, the drug worked remarkably well with his body's natural chemicals to produce a calming effect.

A tap on the door signaled that Phoenix's food had arrived. Deutch opened the door as an unknown government worker placed the trays on the table in front of Phoenix, then turned and left with the same urgency that he had exhibited upon delivering the food.

"Dr. O'Connor, this man needs medical attention. We can't send him out of here through the front. God damn reporters are swarming the front entrance. Take him underground after he eats." Deutch ordered.

"Yes, of course." Dr. O'Connor watched Phoenix, making sure he didn't collapse again.

Phoenix rolled his eyes to the side and studied the director. He slowly sat up in the chair and pulled three trays loaded with a variety of meats toward him. The famished soldier picked up a fork and began shoveling chunks of chicken, fish, and beef into his mouth, savoring each bite. His headache and mind fog began to dissipate as his body refueled and returned to a stable condition. Although he was still under the influence of the Valium injection, the drug's potency would not linger long.

"Mr. Deutch, it's my understanding that you all wanted me transported to Alaska, where I would become a part of the HAARP program's research. Is that correct?" Phoenix wiped his mouth with the corner of his sleeve after his search for a napkin proved useless.

Deutch took a breath and cleared his throat. "Sergeant Major, we transported you to a remote area in Alaska where we believed you would be hidden from anyone wanting to cause you harm."

Phoenix chuckled, then slammed his fist on the table. "Star Gate wasn't your only gig. You sent me there to kill me. You sent me there to study me like a fucking lab rat at HAARP until you could arrange my death in Bosnia, didn't you, Director?"

The director stepped back. "No! You were there. You saw it. You were sent to Srebrenica because nobody else could get those hostages out of there!"

"Who planted the IED's, Mr. Deutch? Who fucking planted the IEDs?"

"What the hell are you talking about?" The director shook his head, looking stunned, his eyes fiery and his brows furrowed.

"I'm talking about the research. I know what you've been doing all along. All of you. I don't know how many of you are behind this, but I will not be a part of your damn cloning program." Phoenix lifted another chunk of meat to his mouth. He relished the taste of prime rib and maintained calm while the director wrestled with visible unease.

Phoenix still had the upper hand, only because the feds had not yet developed a way to penetrate a human mind. It was the only source of privacy that he still had. The privacy of his thoughts. But if Russia and the USA could develop a way to clone their respective superhumans, mind control and invasion would become a future reality.

"Sergeant Major, the research behind human cloning didn't start with you. It's been going on for years. If you think that---

"Your research at Stanford Institute is flawed, Mr. Deutch." Phoenix interrupted.

The director darted his eyes toward the doctor, who now glared at Phoenix through squinted eyes. The doctor was stoic as he waited for Phoenix to continue. O'Connor realized that there was nothing that Phoenix could not penetrate if he willed it. Because Phoenix was able to teleport at will, he could be anywhere at any time. There was no way to control him. HAARP had been a last resort and would have worked if the hostage situation in Bosnia had not foiled the plans.

The director finally responded to Phoenix, playing the dumb card. "Which research are you referring to, Sergeant Major?"

Phoenix leaned back in the chair and pushed his plate away from the edge of the table. He pulled a napkin out from under a butter knife resting on the food tray and wiped the corners of his mouth. He then cocked his head to the side and looked at the director. He lifted his index finger in the air and pointed at Deutch as he spoke.

"You people have been studying my type of abilities for years, trying to duplicate the phenomena or manipulate it through lab experiments. Your present research, which involves measuring a soldier's thoughts before he speaks, will cause unnecessary casualties. You are attempting to take a human being and turn them into some sort of robotic war machine that reacts on cue. Humans are not wired that way. We are too complex." Phoenix waited for the doctor's response.

"Our technology is better served in robotics, not a biological living organism." The doctor interjected.

Phoenix nodded.

"The research at the Stanford Institute goes beyond remote viewing, Sergeant Major. If you are referring to the Army's special programs, I must tell you that the latest program has shown great progress, but the technology is not something that we can share. Not even with other scientists that we have contracted to assist in classified projects."

"It won't work," Phoenix stated without resolve.

"And do you think that you have the ability to train our remote viewers? Do you think that you can do a better job than the teams we have in place? You know how to read minds, Sergeant Major. You know how to make things move. But can you teach the skill to others? To those agents whom we have hand-selected and tested to be highly capable of producing the supernatural phenomena? We've put decades of time into our people and these programs. Casting the current research aside as a folly is a pretty arrogant position to take, Sergeant Major."

The sergeant major watched the director and then continued. "Mr. Deutch, arrogance has nothing to do with my position. I make my argument as a man who has lived his lifetime with these supernatural abilities. Abilities that I have strengthened and developed on my own. What you are trying to do is duplicate a natural occurrence that's guaranteed to produce a synthetic outcome. As far as teaching others, I haven't even given that a thought. You people dropped me off in Alaska expecting me to be forgotten, but then I bypassed the door and those sealed files in the bunker's main office. I scanned at least fifty documents pertaining to HAARP and the research being conducted at Stanford. And this idea of moving my ass to Homey Airport, where you expect me to make my new home with a family of fucking genderless green midgets, is utter bullshit."

The doctor looked down at the floor to keep from laughing out loud. The sergeant major's unintended comic relief was well needed in a roomful of angst. O'Connor decided it was a good time to get Phoenix out of there and underground.

"Sergeant Major, we need to get you out of here now. Part of the reason that you were transported to Alaska was to avoid the media. You're too close to the capital. General Monroe fucked us in a nuclear kind of way when he sold this country out to Russia. We need a really good story that we can sell to the media and the world. A story without you in it. Do you understand?" The doctor leaned forward and stared at Phoenix with one eyebrow cocked.

Phoenix flinched, then turned stone cold as he stared back at O'Connor. He read the doctor's thoughts. *They wanted him dead.*

Phoenix cleared his throat before speaking. "Let's get the hell out of here then." The sergeant major stood and turned toward the door.

The doctor pushed his chair back and walked around the table to join Phoenix. Deutch stopped the doctor as Phoenix reached for the door handle. "Take the tunnel out of here. He doesn't need to be seen exiting the building."

The doctor nodded and replied. "Of course."

O'Connor knew what was coming in the next few hours. He wondered if Phoenix had read the thoughts of everyone in the room, or had they been successful at confusing him? Although the doctor was on Phoenix's side and the only person whom he could trust, he had to play the game until Phoenix was capable of taking control. Dr. O'Connor knew that the feds would never be able to control Phoenix. But how far were they willing to go to get what they wanted?

"And get him a damn shower, will you? He smells like piss." Deutch ordered in a disdainful tone.

The doctor ignored the director's arrogant remarks and shut the door behind him. Phoenix looked at Dr. O'Connor as they entered the hallway leading out. The armed guard immediately led them into an elevator. He inserted a key into the elevator's interior panel, then entered a secret code into a numeric pad. The elevator doors shut and began the descent eight stories beneath the earth's surface. For the next 24 hours, Sergeant Major Seth Phoenix would be completely shut off from the outside world and the sole property of the United States of America.

CHAPTER 28

Foreign Intelligence Service Headquarters
Yasenevo, Russia

Special Agent Nikita Oleshun felt the brunt force of an officer's fist against the back of her neck as she fell to the floor. She quickly pushed her hands out in front of her to catch herself before slamming against the hard, polished tiles. Her eyes began to gloss over as her hands now stung from the impact, and she quickly tuned into the silent communication within the minds of those surrounding her.

A trickle of blood dripped down her neck where the officer's fingernail had lanced the delicate skin behind her right earlobe. She was about to be ambushed by the SVR if she didn't act fast. The prime minister and former KGB stood over her, glaring at her through wide eyes that transferred a fatal warning to Russia's most coveted spy. Although the Russian government knew the magnitude of her supernatural capabilities, she had been at the forefront of their research and under their control for more than a decade. And they weren't about to sacrifice a breach of trust even from the likes of her.

Her eyes quickly scanned the area around her, and she saw that she was surrounded by dozens of armed agents whose weapons were now deadlocked on her. She breathed deep and slow, trying to calm herself and lower her blood pressure as she looked down at the barrels of the rifles. If she made any sudden moves, she knew that they would pummel her with bullets and leave her body covered in more holes than a block of Swiss cheese. Her powers were strong, but she wasn't stupid, and she knew better than to test the men before her.

Nikita slowly moved her legs up toward her chest and began to push herself upright. As she began to stand, she looked up and locked stares with the piercing blue eyes of the prime minister. He watched her, unrelenting in his desire for domination. Nikita acknowledged his commanding presence and blinked once. She offered no other sign of submission, instead beginning to mentally record the scene as a computer processes an encrypted message. As her mind raced to sort through the incoming data, a plan of escape began to formulate. She felt her adrenal glands spike, releasing the coveted hormone that keeps her alive during recovery. Her body jerked in response, and at that moment, she parted her lips to speak.

"Prime Minister," Nikita said to Putin in a tone that invited dialogue between them. She refused to remove her eyes from his but continued her stance with a softened look as she waited for his response.

Putin breathed in and stepped back, turning his head to the side as he sized her up, a move that defined his displeasure and foreshadowed the tone to come. "Did you think that you could fool us, Nikita? Did you think that we would not know?"

Nikita remained still, not daring to move an inch. Her body became ravaged with fear as she stood painfully stiff before him. *What if Putin didn't believe her?*

"There was an explosion, Mr. Putin. I saw the American. Sergeant Major Seth Phoenix. I saw him enter the building, and I saw the hostages being removed, but--"

Nikita waited. Putin turned and looked back at the president and the agents surrounding him with pointed weapons. He then leaned forward toward her. "And your mission was to gather intelligence about this Phoenix. Your mission was to collect a sample of his DNA." His tone was barely above a whisper as he spat the words in Russian and clenched his teeth.

Then, without warning, he yelled, slamming his fist in the air. "And you brought us nothing! You brought us nothing!" The prime minister repeated, causing Nikita to flinch. She felt a drop of spittle land against her cheek.

"The explosion—it—there was nothing left. The American was still inside." Nikita hesitated, stumbling over her words, but her tone sounded convincing. *How could they know if she had communicated with Phoenix?* She had been tracking Phoenix alone.

Prime Minister Vladimir Putin became quiet. He studied her. Just minutes before, the Russian agent had exited the Mil M24 that had transported her to the Russian intelligence and espionage headquarters situated in the center of a Russian forest in Yasenevo. He had watched her from the windows of the second-floor office as she exited the aircraft. He watched her body language as she made her way to the doors leading into the Y-shaped campus that housed some of the most sophisticated intelligence systems in the world.

The country's most skilled intelligence officers had tracked Oleshun during the explosion, and Putin had been briefed on her movements outside of Srebrenica. The Russians trusted no one. Not even their own mother. Regardless of what Nikita Oleshun meant to the Russian government, she was treated as a potential threat capable of exposing Russia's most guarded secrets.

Putin stood before her with his hands clasped in front of him. "We know you were there." He stated matter-of-factly. "We also know that you hid out in a cave about a half mile in the hills overlooking Srebrenica."

Nikita said nothing but continued to stare into the prime minister's eyes. She guarded her reactions with extreme caution, careful not to reveal any telling body language in response to Putin's claims. The prime minister's remarks now confirmed her worst fear. She realized that the Russians had planted a tracking device on her body during one of her remote viewing sessions. She felt the flow of wet blood that had oozed onto her throat, but she hesitated to check the source. She suspected that the device was located somewhere on her head, and she knew that she had to locate it and remove it, but not without a plan of escape first. The SVR would be watching every move she made, even the number of times she chewed her food and emptied her bladder.

Nikita spoke in a hoarse voice. Her throat produced a scratchy, exhausted tone. "Yes, I used the cave for surveillance before I went in, and then I escaped to the same location after the explosion. Phoenix was inside when the Serbs stormed from the back of the building. There must have been a dozen homemade bomb devices." Nikita shook her head while remembering the magnitude of the explosion, then continued. "I got out of there just as I watched the last of the American agents running for cover. There is no way he could have survived such a massive explosion. It leveled parts of that building." Nikita's tone was straightforward and showed no signs of deception, but the president wasn't convinced. He cut his eyes toward Putin and put his hand over his lips, resting his chin in his palm as he paused for a moment and contemplated what the special agent had just told them. She had been convincing, but President Yeltsin wanted Nikita to understand the consequences of betrayal. He straightened his stature and then turned to walk away from the scene. He took two steps, then halted and addressed the prime minister.

"Mr. Putin, please inform Ms. Oleshun of Russia's expectations for her. And make sure she understands."

A cold chill swept over Nikita. At that moment, she vowed to escape the country or die trying, but staying there was no longer an option.

"Yes, Mr. President, of course."

Putin waited for the door to close behind Yeltsin, then turned back toward Nikita. He stepped close toward her and faced her. He motioned for one of the agents to join his side. A tall, dark Russian man stepped forward and lowered his weapon. Putin gave the man his order and spoke under his breath, hoping that Nikita would not hear him. The dark-haired Russian then stepped forward. Although he was not touching her, he leaned toward her right side and bent close to her ear, his lips almost touching her earlobe. He spoke in a cold and malevolent tone.

"If you're lying, we're going to take that superhuman brain of yours and feed it to the pigs. Do you understand?"

Nikita's heart raced, and her scalp began to tingle as her telekinetic energy spiked. She wanted to kill him right there, but she would have to fight all of them. They outnumbered her in this moment. They had the upper hand. For the time being.

Nikita's mouth fell slightly open, and she breathed deeply. She nodded and muttered the word, "Yes."

"You can get out of here now, Ms. Oleshun. We'll be in touch."

Nikita let out a quiet sigh and closed her eyes, then quickly opened them. She began to walk toward the door as the army of agents moved aside while she exited the room. Putin followed close behind her and instructed the commander in charge to deliver Ms. Oleshun to her apartment, located just two miles away.

As the SVR agent escorted her to a Russian military transport vehicle, she attempted telepathic communication with Sergeant Major Seth Phoenix, now located eight stories beneath the earth's surface.

CHAPTER 29

Nikita's body was stiff, and she didn't dare move during the two-mile ride to her home. She stared ahead as if in a catatonic state and continued to use her mental powers to push through time and space as she attempted to reach Sergeant Major Seth Phoenix. She called out to him through her telepathic channels and repeated the urgent message to ensure it was delivered. Phoenix must hear her. He must be made aware that she would be arriving in the city by his name. She would be flying into Phoenix, Arizona. It was a nonstop flight from Russia to a destination close to where the sergeant major was reportedly being moved. She had telepathically picked up data that indicated Seth Phoenix was going to be transported to Homey Airport. If it was right, she wanted to be there. She knew the sergeant major's intentions. She had seen them through their exchange back in the hillside cave in Srebrenica. And she wanted the same freedoms, but she was now running for her life.

She heard mental static and realized she was tuning into the underground tunnel where Phoenix was now resting. Mental images zoomed in and out of her brain's visual cortex, recording

Phoenix's sensory data that translated to his current moods and physiological status. Nikita took a slow, deep breath, careful to keep it unnoticed by her escorts. Her eyes narrowed as if she was blinded by a bright light as she deciphered the information that she was receiving. Phoenix was in restoration. She observed the past hour of his time in the tunnel and concluded that he had been fed and questioned by a government official overseeing his medical care. She watched a snapshot in time as the doctor started an IV in Phoenix's left arm. And then just as she was about to call out to the sergeant major, the driver made a sudden turn that broke her train of concentration. She was within yards of her home's front door. The sudden movement of the SUV caused her body to slide over, almost touching the Russian agent, who now turned and glared at her. His eyes were as cold as ice and issued a warning meant not only to intimidate the female spy, but also to dominate and declare his self-proclaimed supremacy. She quickly slid back to the right and sat up against the passenger side door. She jerked her head around and stared straight ahead as she attempted a final and urgent call to Sergeant Major Seth Phoenix.

Like a radio blasting a warning signal, Nikita's voice raced through an invisible network. While Phoenix reclined on a cot inside the bunker's medical hall, her signals traveled faster than the speed of sound until they crossed over, penetrating outside barriers and passing directly into his brain's sensory canals. Just as the last snippets of Nikita's message rocketed forward, the sound of her voice caused his eyes to fly open and his feet to lift off the chair.

In a flash, Phoenix looked all around the room. Nikita's voice had come through like a loud siren. In fact, the sound of her voice seemed to bounce off the walls, creating an echo. He wondered whether the doctor had witnessed the same phenomenon he had just experienced. But the doctor seemed oblivious to it as he continued writing in an unidentified file. Phoenix then settled back onto the chair and listened. He waited, and he listened. And then in a split second, he answered her back.

Near the Moscow Metro, Yasenevo

The driver turned into the apartment community parking lot and stopped near the entrance to Nikita's front door. The area was well obscured by the night sky, but the agents already knew exactly which apartment Nikita lived in and even how many steps it took to reach her front door from the sidewalk.

The six-foot-four, two-hundred-thirty-five-pound Russian loyalist and foreign spy slammed the gear shift into park and hastily got out of the car as the other agent opened the back door and reached into the vehicle, pulling Nikita out by the arm and onto her feet. Both men stood behind her and motioned for her to leave, but they watched her like a hawk until she entered the building. The men then turned, got back into the SUV, and drove away, but not far. She didn't doubt for a second that she was being tracked, not only by the device that she was about to remove but also through other means of surveillance. They were watching her apartment from all four directions and even the sky.

Once inside, Nikita immediately began preparing for departure. A secret and urgent escape that would likely get her killed unless she was able to remove the small device implanted beneath her skin. The Russians had managed to plant it behind her right earlobe, in the soft crevice of skin folds. It was a smart location for a tracking device since she had not detected its presence until the brunt force of the Russian officer's fist had loosened and cracked open the skin. Even during her daily bathing regimen, she had not detected the tiny, wire-looking apparatus that fit snugly in the back bend of her ear.

The top-secret agent now stood in front of the bathroom sink. She traced her index finger along the right ear, and after a few tries, she detected it beneath her skin. She winced as she bent her earlobe forward and leaned closer to the mirror so that she could examine its location. Her eyes widened as she saw the wire that had been tracking her every movement. It was there, just barely visible under a thin layer of skin and blood. As she examined the area, she realized that the device had been placed there so easily that it was no surprise it had gone unnoticed. She had not even felt it being surgically implanted.

Nikita flicked open a pocketknife and pricked the skin with the wire tip. A small trickle of blood oozed out of the opening that now exposed the end of the wire as Nikita used a pair of tweezers to grasp hold of it and pull it away from the skin. She had to be prepared to make her exit as soon as the wire was removed because the Russians would know that she had located the tracking device. Nikita laid the wire down and quickly placed a tissue against the small hole, applying pressure to stop the bleeding. She then grabbed a backpack and stuffed it with a fake ID, a change of clothes, and a box of protein snacks. She then hauled ass toward the back door. Every move she made had to be three steps ahead of the Russians stalking her. She had to use her abilities to know everything they were thinking and planning. She even had to know the precise moment when her stalkers were sneaking a few blinks or a glance down at the ground that would allow her to slip by unnoticed. And at this fateful moment, she seized the opportunity when the Russian hiding at the corner of the apartment complex looked down at the ground and rubbed his nose. At that moment, she scurried down two flights of stairs, unscathed and undetected. The next few hours would become the ultimate test of her abilities as she boarded a plane for the Land of Dreams.

CHAPTER 30

Sheremetyevo International Airport
Moscow, Russia

Nikita quickly pushed the taxicab door open and exited the back seat after paying the cab fare for the forty-minute ride. Her feet moved with phenomenal speed as she zipped past security guards. For every blink or distraction they yielded to, she was right there reading it seconds before it happened. The minor infractions allowed her to escape past them without being seen or heard. She knew the Russians were now scrambling to intercept her, and if they succeeded, she would be dead.

She blended in with the hundreds of travelers all hurrying to catch their flights. She raced to the ticket kiosk and rushed to purchase a one-way flight to Phoenix, Arizona. She pulled out a fake ID and a credit card in the same name to make the purchase. Within seconds, the transaction was processed, and a paper ticket was dispensed. Nikita wasted no time and headed straight for the security point.

She waited in line and mentally tuned in to her surroundings. She detected no approaching interference, but she suspected that it would be only hours away, if not sooner. But just as she felt a moment of relief from her angst, a flash of insight burst forth before her eyes and alerted her to footsteps running steadfast toward her. She jerked around and made a dash for the restroom, leaving her place in line empty for the man behind her. She breathed fast as she walked into a stall and stood on top of the toilet seat. She slammed the door shut and knelt, closing her eyes and reading the scene, deciphering the energy of the uniformed men coming through the airport. *Security guards. Four of them. Searching for a suspect wanted in a crime committed just twenty-four hours before.*

Nikita opened her eyes and leaned her head back, her lips pursed with nervous tension. She had to remain calm. *Somehow.* She stepped down from the toilet and opened the bathroom door. Then immediately jerked backward as someone rushed around the corner to another bathroom stall.

She waited and stood still, rubbing her fingertips against the temple of her head as she concentrated once again. But this time, she focused on the interior of her apartment, attempting to detect any movement. She was stunned as she remotely viewed her living quarters. Not one thing had been disturbed since she escaped down two flights of stairs. But she knew that it wouldn't be long. She saw the SVR agents still standing watch at the property's front and rear exits. They had not been alerted by headquarters yet, but she knew that as soon as someone realized the wire had been removed, a hunt bigger than hell itself would ensue. And it was coming. Within minutes.

The Russian Foreign Service Agent walked out of the stall and exited the restroom. She didn't bother to survey the area as she took her place back in line again and placed her backpack on the conveyor belt. She waited until the guard motioned for her to walk through, then handed over her ticket for one last pass. Then, without hesitation, he motioned for her to move forward. Nikita had managed to bypass security points. By now, the Foreign Intelligence Headquarters was most likely discovering the missing link to Nikita Oleshun and ordering her to be assassinated on sight.

Nikita hurried, her feet almost airborne across the airport's high-gloss polished floors. She skipped three steps at a time up the escalator and made the final turn toward her boarding gate. As she neared the area, she saw the gate attendant lift the microphone to his mouth and announce the final boarding call. Within two swift steps, Nikita Oleshun was passing in front of him, her ticket in hand as she stepped across the threshold and into the plane's main cabin. As she took a seat near the back of the plane, she took a deep breath and sighed, exhaling in silence. Then she whispered to herself. *Still alive. Nineteen hours to go.*

CHAPTER 31

Sergeant Major Seth Phoenix jerked awake and rolled over at the sound of splitting wood. He swung his legs off the reclining chair and looked from side to side, his eyes wild and his movements fast and furious as he surveyed his surroundings. But all was peaceful in the underground tunnel beneath the headquarters of the Department of Homeland Security. He looked down at his arm and noticed the bandage that had been placed where the IV had been inserted a few hours before he fell into a deep sleep after sending Nikita Oleshun a final telepathic message. Phoenix cautiously walked to the edge of the door and peered out. He listened to the silence in the bunker and realized that he had been left alone.

Without warning, another loud crash echoed in his mind. He stood straight and began to investigate the rooms in the bunker. He was receiving intel from another location, but it wasn't at Fort Meade. He stopped near the exit door where Dr. O'Connor had led him into the tunnel and froze as he zeroed in on the communication being transmitted. Like a fading radio signal, he heard the Russians messaging each other before the final blow that ripped a door off its hinges. He watched the scene through clairvoyant means as the Russian agents stormed Nikita Oleshun's apartment. They jerked open closet doors and ransacked cabinets filled with her belongings that she never intended to come back for.

Phoenix knew that he was watching the event in real time. It was happening now, and he heard the Russian commands as they ordered her killed on sight. Complete and total chaos ensued as the Russians now scrambled to find her. Dozens of agents scattered in multiple directions, with at least ten agents heading with perpetual lightning speed for the Sheremetyevo International Airport, but it was too late. The 747 had already lifted and was now within minutes of crossing into U.S. airspace.

Fifty-five miles from the Alaskan border

Nikita jerked in her seat as she received telepathic intel from the sergeant major who was now attempting to communicate with her from thousands of miles away. She leaned forward and viewed the scene across the aisles of the plane's interior cabin. Most of the passengers were now sleeping or occupied with movies and reading. All was quiet. She then leaned back and rested her head against the headrest. She closed her eyes as she envisioned Phoenix standing before her.

Using her clairaudient abilities, she listened to the sergeant major's raspy voice and southern dialect as he ordered her to stay put when the plane landed in Arizona. Although his message was short, it was precise, and there was no misunderstanding of his warning. As Phoenix transmitted his final thoughts across an invisible network, Nikita Oleshun's body became rigid, and a cold chill swept over her. Russia didn't want the U.S. to know about Nikita's defection. They would take great care to preserve their secrets, and they were no longer interested in her return. Nikita mouthed her thoughts. *A Russian assassin would be waiting.*

CHAPTER 32

Hours later.
Phoenix Sky Harbor International Airport
Phoenix, Arizona

Sergeant Major Seth Phoenix waited for his supernatural match. The plane carrying the Russian special agent was due to land within minutes, and Phoenix was watching the tarmac through a ten-foot-high window at the terminal's gate. Phoenix left nothing behind when he exited the tunnel and made his way off the base at Fort Meade. And he didn't bother to tell anyone where he was going. He zipped past people, causing mild delays for them as he instigated annoying mishaps. In order to avoid being seen by the front staff at HSA, Phoenix sent a shock wave of air toward the security guard, sending the man's eyeglasses off his face and to the floor. As the guard scrambled to retrieve his necessary spectacles, Phoenix zipped past. Within seconds and with a supernatural disguise that only he could maneuver, he was gone and out of sight before anyone realized he was headed for Arizona. At least that's what Phoenix was hoping, since he was expected to stay underground for twenty-four hours under the doctor's care before being transported to Homey Airport the following morning. Top secret officials were then expected to inform the sergeant major of his role in the current military research programs. But Phoenix was already receiving fragments of information that were coming through as broken radio signals. It was still enough for him to make out what was transpiring as he stood waiting for Russia's number one kill target.

The 747 could now be seen at low altitudes as it made its way past the red Arizona mountains. Phoenix's pale blue eyes began to glow as he locked sights on the massive plane with its landing gear now open and ready to hit the pavement. His supernatural sight revealed Nikita sitting near the back of the plane. She appeared calm and collected. He sent her a telepathic signal that he had arrived and would be waiting as she exited the plane.

The Delta airliner made a smooth landing on the runway, with only minimal forward thrust, as the plane abruptly slowed and entered the gate. Phoenix began to pace the floor. He walked back and forth around the area and away from the line of people that had now congregated near the ticket counter, but he never took his eyes off the crowd. He watched them and invaded their thoughts as he practiced supernatural surveillance on each person within thirty feet of the exit door. He didn't detect any possible interference. Contrary to his expectations, the scene seemed almost surreal, leaving him momentarily confused and curious. There was no CIA there. No FBI. No cops or security interference. Although Phoenix was picking up bits of future conversations, it had been broken into fragments and was difficult to discern. The doctor and the CIA knew he could read their every move, but Phoenix was being played. The White House knew about Nikita Oleshun and that she was landing at Phoenix Sky Harbor International Airport.

The plane's door was thrust open, and travelers began to make their way down the ramp toward the terminal. Phoenix knew Nikita would be one of the last to de-board the plane, but he still scanned every person as each one passed through the door. At this point, Phoenix assessed every person he encountered as a potential enemy.

Just then, Nikita Oleshun stepped foot across the threshold and into the terminal. Her body tingled as her senses soared into high alert. She moved quickly through the crowd, cautiously, until Phoenix suddenly stepped forward and locked eyes with her. Nikita stopped dead still for a brief moment as she stared into her American ally's face. Her own expressions were revealing enough without the need to penetrate her thoughts. The two of them shared a chemistry beyond the biological engineering of their supernatural makeup. And it was obvious.

Phoenix tore his eyes away and quickly motioned for her to follow.   There wasn't time for romantic interludes, even though he felt it all the way to his loins. Nikita wasted no time and fell in behind Phoenix as they made their way through the airport terminal and toward the escalators leading to the baggage and claims division. The two of them hurriedly placed their feet on the moving steps. She noticed the suspended airplane hanging from the ceiling, set against a backdrop of a built-in stone waterfall. The scene was one that she would never forget as she stood close to Phoenix.

As the escalator neared the ground level of the airport, Phoenix skipped a couple of steps and moved fast toward the outside doors. He then paused and turned to Nikita. Phoenix whispered; his words were hushed but precise.

"We have a greeter waiting to meet us."

Nikita nodded. "Russian assassin."

"We have to reach Homey Airport."

Phoenix knew that they had to remain almost invisible to the people around them, and it wasn't safe to use any of their telekinetic abilities even if they had to. Although the scene appeared to be clear, he knew he had to meet Nikita Oleshun's enemy in the open. He had to drag him out. If the assassin was armed as he suspected, Nikita would need help. The supernatural Russian agent was a walking bullseye, and a secret Russian assassin on American soil wasn't going home without a kill.

"What now?" Nikita took a deep breath and focused on the parking garage ahead of them.

Phoenix pushed the door open and immediately scanned the area with X-ray vision. He raised his hand in the air and motioned for her to follow. "In the car."

The base was a good eight-hour drive, including restroom stops, from the heart of Arizona. If they managed to stay alive and make it to the entrance of Homey Airport, they could consider themselves home free. The base was one of the most guarded installations in the entire world. But any unauthorized individual who stepped one foot across the restricted line could set off an ambush worse than the FBI's slaughter of Bonnie and Clyde, who took one hundred thirty rounds of steel-jacketed bullets. The only thing worse than being killed at Area 51 was being caught alive and sentenced to a federal prison where the bad boys would mind fuck a person until they were ready to kill them.

Phoenix knew that the White House wanted him kept alive regardless of the aggravation he had caused. He was on the run to save a Russian defector who had become an important ally and a trusted friend. As long as he stayed within the homeland, he was still considered a government spy with a negotiable future. That's what the president and the CIA wanted. A negotiation with the supernatural spy. If Nikita Oleshun did what CIA Director Deutch anticipated her to do, she would gladly accept an offer that would end her days on the run.

Dr. O'Connor and the research team at Stanford Institute would continue the military's paranormal research under a secret umbrella that the CIA would no longer make available to any Congressional committee. The project would continue as a black operation with no access outside the team's main operatives. And there would be a scarce paper trail detailing the program's progress.

The sergeant major and Russian secret spy entered the airport parking garage and found the Dodge Charger Phoenix had picked up from the car rental downstairs. They got in the car and slammed the doors shut, not wasting a second before speeding out around the corner and onto the highway leading straight to the Nevada desert.

The two agents were quiet for a moment, consumed by the reality of the present as they fixed their sights on the road ahead. Phoenix and Oleshun shared the gifts of telepathy, telekinesis, and clairvoyance, but none of these abilities enabled them to change a future occurrence. What it could do was allow them a chance to change a future outcome if they had time to intervene. The Russian assassin would be waiting, and Nikita now feared the confrontation. She knew he would be armed with an arsenal. Enough to kill a small army of men.

In an instant, Nikita felt a chilling revelation creep upon her, slamming into her mental faculties. She jerked around and looked at Phoenix, who met her glance.

"He's just ahead of us." Nikita's eyes were wide. Her hands trembled as she positioned her fingertips against both sides of her temples, massaging them in a circular motion.

Phoenix's eyes were squinting as he stared ahead. He zeroed in on the road ahead of him, and then, without warning, he yelled out, his body now tense as he swerved to miss the oncoming car.

"Oh, fuck! No, he's here now! Get down!"

The Russian assassin slammed into the front driver's side of the black Dodge Charger. The sound of crushing metal and screeching tires burned into Nikita's ears as she struggled to gain control of her body, being slung about. She grabbed the side door handle as her head slammed against the glass window. Her mouth gaped open, and tears streamed down her cheeks from the pain of the impact. A trickle of blood escaped just beneath her brow, and she quickly reached up and placed her hand against the fresh wound now pulsing with pain. She pulled her hand away and inspected her wet fingers, now covered in bright, crimson blood. Rage began to consume her as she viewed her own life force and the reality of a certain death staring her in the face. Instead of fear, she felt anger bubbling up inside of her, and at that moment, she wanted revenge. Revenge for the loss of years she gave the Russian government, the sacrifice, and the dedication that now was about to be extinguished. Time seemed to slow down, creating the sensation of slow motion, yet everything was actually happening in split-second speed.

"Send a shock wave!" Phoenix shouted.

"A what?" Nikita shouted back in confusion. She then pulled her knees up to her chest and turned to face the back of the car, looking out the rear window.

"Blast the fuck out of him!" Phoenix shouted, his tone now more urgent than ever as he swerved to the other lane of the highway. The assassin was fast gaining on him and was within inches of ramming him from behind.

Phoenix looked in the rearview mirror as the white 4x4 Chevy inched closer. "What the fuck?" The sergeant major struggled to keep his eyes on the truck as he zipped back and forth between the truck and the road. He noticed something situated in the passenger seat and tried to determine what the assassin had posted there. Just then, his mouth fell open as the assassin placed his fingers on the trigger of a rocket aimed dead at them.

"Get down!" Phoenix shouted, slamming the gas pedal to the floor as the car's engine roared and accelerated them forward. Phoenix fought to maintain control of the car, desperately trying to avoid a crash. But the back and forth across the lanes and the hundred-mile-an-hour speeds were leading him and his supernatural accomplice to their own grave if he didn't eliminate the Russian killer now.

At that very moment, Nikita released a supersonic wave toward the assailant. The invisible mega-force rocked the truck, crushing the front grille as the killer squeezed the release button. The rocket launched from its base, shattering the front windshield as the assailant's body fell backward.

Phoenix worked furiously to spin the car around in the opposite direction, and his palms felt the burn of the leather steering wheel as he jerked and slid it counterclockwise. The deadly rocket zoomed past, headed for the middle of nowhere until the sound of its detonation pierced the ears of its survivors. The car screeched to a sudden stop, with heat from the tires sending a cloud of smoke into the air.

Phoenix acted fast as he shook off the aftershock and pushed against the driver's side door that was now crushed in. The door latch was broken in half, and Phoenix was trapped as the Russian assailant marched in speedy haste toward him, rifle in hand and ready to fire. Phoenix pushed both his palms forward. His supernatural power pulsated forward, sending the car door flying into the air. Nikita rushed to exit the passenger side and shield herself away from the assailant's view, but just as she knelt beside the right front of the car, the assailant hurled an explosive device that had been laced with a paralyzing agent designed to disable her. One breath of the toxic chemical and she would be rendered helpless, if not dead.

Phoenix was too late. The metal canister clinked as it landed on the asphalt near the car. A putrid smell of burning rubber escaped as the vapors filled the air, indicating that the gas wasn't in its purest form. The killer was using chemical weapons of mass destruction known as Sarin, a deadly nerve agent that would destroy Nikita Oleshun's central nervous system within seconds. She would have no defense against this type of weapon, and the Russian assassin would have the dead body that he came for.

Phoenix jumped in the air and sailed over the hood of the car. His feet barely hit the ground as he grabbed Nikita by the arm. In one swift move, he threw her over his shoulder and raced away with expeditious speed. Even though Phoenix had moved with fury, both of the supernatural agents had been mildly exposed as they inhaled the vapors while fleeing the area. And

Phoenix knew the chemicals' effects were now just seconds away.

He slowed to a stop and eased Nikita off his back. The mind-reading spy coughed and looked at Phoenix with a cocky smile. "Many thanks, sergeant major. Looks like we're even now."

Phoenix chose to ignore the remark and shook his head. He pointed ahead at the abandoned vehicles. The empty tin canisters that carried the deadly nerve gas lay in the middle of the road, and the Russian killer appeared to have vanished. Phoenix knew better, but he didn't want to admit to Nikita that they might not make it to Homey Airport. The Sarin that they had been exposed to was twenty-six times more deadly than cyanide, and Phoenix's pupils had already begun to constrict. He then took Nikita by the hand and lifted her chin with his other hand, holding her face at eye level with his own. He looked into the pale blue eyes that matched his own.

Nikita had to catch herself as her legs grew weak. She wanted to embrace the sergeant major at that moment. The moment when the veil had been lifted, she was allowed to walk through a door that had been closed to all others until now. For a brief moment, he let her see and feel the tenderness of his heart before he resumed a sergeant major's posture. As Phoenix pulled away and released her hand from his, he issued a final and deadly command.

"Let's kill this bastard."

Nikita stood beside him, ready to join forces. The two of them faced north and scanned the area searching for the assassin who now stalked them from a few yards away. He had managed to escape the airborne vapors and was now hiding out in the bed of the truck. The assassin picked up a Browning .50 caliber machine gun and pointed the barrel with a dead-on aim at Nikita

Oleshun. The assassin tightened his fingers around the trigger and squeezed.

Phoenix tasted the salty liquid that dripped from his nose and eyelids. He then moved closer to Nikita, and in one swift motion, the two of them joined forces, their arms stretched outward, palms facing outward as Phoenix screamed, "Now!"

Although their bodies were weakening from exposure to Sarin, the two equals emitted electromagnetic pulses that produced wind speeds of up to 100 miles per hour. Nikita's eyes resonated with psychedelic blue while Phoenix's eyes glowed pale blue, almost white. Nikita's head hurt, and sweat soaked her shirt as she pummeled her energies forward. Until she heard the bullets. In her extraordinary awareness and heightened hearing ability, she heard the bullets before they were even expelled from the barrel of the .50 caliber gun.

Nikita fell to the ground. Seth Phoenix felt Nikita's energy dissipate, and he swiftly joined her as the two dodged bullets that penetrated the weakened electromagnetic wall they had built together.

From a distance, the Russian assassin felt the force of their explosion, but the winds were dying fast without a continual onslaught from the two superheroes. The roar of the magnetic blast sent the assassin off his feet and into the air. He was hurled almost thirty feet away from the truck, where he landed with a bone-breaking thud against the concrete ground. He scrambled to get up and reclaim any still-functional weapons in the back of the truck. But just as he placed a hand on the truck's tailgate and pulled himself up, he felt a powerful wind circling above him, and he heard the familiar thunderous sounds of helicopter blades.

Phoenix felt the ground vibrating beneath him. The helicopter blades chopping through the air caused him to automatically cover his head and ears. He slowly lifted his eyes upward and saw the symbol on the side of the chopper. It was a Lakota, a rescue chopper used for Med-Vac. United States Army. And following its lead was an Apache air cavalry. Where there was one, there would be more. He rolled over and touched Nikita. She was still alert but showed dangerous symptomatic signs of Sarin poisoning. Her eyes were watery, and her mouth drooled. Phoenix slowly got up on his knees and waved his hand in the air at the chopper now descending nearby.

The assassin lay frozen in the bed of the truck as he watched Phoenix rise to his knees. It was now or never. He had to kill them both. He had to fulfill the mission. He knew he would die at the hands of the Americans, but not without suffering the death of their own Sergeant Major Seth Phoenix and the Russian agent turned trader.

He scrambled out of the truck and ran fast and hard toward Phoenix. He tucked the Russian PP-19 Bizon on his shoulder as he readied himself to fire the 9mm rounds. And then with a fierce and sadistic roar, he charged forward, emptying the gun clip.

Phoenix fell over, his body now resting against Nikita as the Russian assassin stormed toward him. Hovering above them inside the chopper were two snipers positioned at the side door, rifles in hand. The snipers expedited the kill with a fury as they released an onslaught of rounds from the barrel of an AWC-G2 rifle. The Russian assailant's arms flew out as his body appeared to convulse before he fell dead.

Within seconds, the chopper was on the ground, and a rescue team of four soldiers dressed in typical camouflage gear exited the aircraft. One by one, they jumped to the ground and rushed to Phoenix's side. The two-person teams quickly lifted the sergeant major and Nikita Oleshun onto a gurney. The men then hurried to the chopper and placed the two agents in the rear, where emergency medical response was now administered.

With the two most coveted humans in the world now back in the U.S. military's hands, the chopper blades sped up, and the bird headed straight for Homey Airport. Within seconds before the chopper could clear the area, a government "cleaner" was on-site to remove the Russian assassin's dead body. The "cleaner" dressed to look like a banker in a navy-blue jacket and khaki pants slid the van door open and lifted the body into the rear of the vehicle. He then slammed the door shut, jumped back into the driver's seat, and sped away. He had a job to finish in another location, but when it was done, the Russian assassin's body would be disintegrated along with any history of his existence in the USA. It would be as if he had vanished into oblivion. Without even a trace.

CHAPTER 33

Inside Homey Airport, aka AREA 51
0607 hours

Nikita Oleshun opened her eyes and moved them from side to side as she surveyed her surroundings. She was now inside the compound of Area 51, the most guarded and highly classified military base in the entire world. Unauthorized people were not allowed within miles of the installation, and no trespassers had ever lived to talk about their discoveries.

The military had somewhat successfully denied its existence for more than four decades, but there was no denying the base's developmental programs that included the research and design of new weapon systems, otherwise known as black projects. This was the Stanford Institute's real secret. The living and breathing products of Dr. Nathaniel O'Connor's team and their experimentation. Star Gate had only been a speck on a grid map of secret ops that not only the United States Army but also all other branches of the military commanded. It was a combined effort in military science and a race to see who finished first in the highly classified paranormal studies of the human mind.

Nikita looked down toward her feet. She was covered by an army-green bedsheet. She turned her head from side to side, testing her ability to move, then drummed her fingers against the mattress. *Everything seems to be intact.* She then lifted her hands and rested them on her abdomen. She ran her hands across her pelvic area and immediately realized that she was naked underneath the sheet. She jerked her head off the bed and frantically looked around the room. As her eyes darted around the area, she noticed Phoenix on the other side of a wall with only a window separating them. He appeared to be awake, but resting.

Nikita then reached back toward her head and felt her hair. She could tell that it had been wet. She smelled the skin on her arms and detected a faint odor like some sort of detergent. The naked mystery was solved now as she realized that they had washed their bodies down after the Sarin exposure.

The sergeant major sensed someone staring at him from across the room. He turned his head to the left and met her eyes. He then casually lifted his left hand in the air and waved "hello" as if he didn't have a care in the world.

Nikita's face broke into a smile as she let out a laugh under her breath. She then touched the temple of her head with her first two fingers, signaling to Phoenix that she was attempting telepathic communication. Nikita wasn't certain if it was clear for her and Phoenix to talk aloud, and she wanted to know if they were now at Homey Airport.

Phoenix studied Nikita and listened to her thoughts as the two of them stared into each other's eyes. He heard her and responded with one slow blink. Then he answered her, and she received his response in short snippets.

Affirmative. Homey.

The Russian spy then offered a cute eye roll as she sent another telepathic message. This time, she wanted to know where the hell her clothes were.

The sergeant major looked stunned and patted the bedsheet covering him. He stared back with that "oh shit" kind of look as he glanced around searching for his own. He then raised his eyebrows and shrugged his shoulders before he peeled the bedsheet back, revealing his partially nude body. He then got out of bed and stood with his back to Nikita as she stared in disbelief at the sergeant major's no-nonsense approach to modesty.

His perfectly chiseled, round ass now faced her as her cheeks flushed pink during a moment of admiration. The sergeant major then raised his arm in the air. He made a circular motion with his hand, signaling for her to get out of bed while his back was turned, giving her some privacy.

Nikita reacted in an instant as she slung her legs to one side and lifted herself off the bed. She pulled the bedsheet around her body as she now examined a panel of flashing lights and low-toned beeping equipment near the opposite side of the room. But just as she placed one foot forward, a male voice rang out from the doorway.

"Your clothes?" The unidentified man in a white coat and wire-rimmed spectacles stepped forward and handed them over.

Nikita looked down at the freshly pressed, folded pair of Army fatigues, with a matching shirt, boots, and underwear appropriate for a woman. She offered no comment, instead nodding and accepting the clothing. The man then turned toward the window, where Phoenix was now standing, fully dressed, observing Nikita's interaction with Dr. Richard Scott, one of the leading research scientists at Homey Airport, and unknown to anyone outside Area 51.

Dr. Scott acknowledged Phoenix with a head nod and then stepped around the dividing wall and into Phoenix's room. The 6'1", blond-haired man almost stood toe to toe with Phoenix's 6'3" stature. He extended his hand in a welcoming gesture and waited for Phoenix to accept his handshake. Phoenix studied the scientist with curiosity and caution but did not hesitate to reciprocate the man's gesture. As their hands met, the scientist greeted the sergeant major with instructions.

"Welcome, Sergeant Major Seth Phoenix. We've been waiting for you and your Russian accomplice to recover from that near-death event yesterday. Please join us now, down the hall in Room 33. Your friends are waiting for you." The scientist squeezed Phoenix's hand and smiled before releasing it and turning to walk out.

Phoenix was speechless, his brows furrowed as he assessed the scientist's peculiar words. He felt as if he had just stepped into the twilight zone. *Your friends are waiting for you. What the hell did that mean?*

Phoenix looked through the wide window separating him from Nikita and motioned for her to join him at the doorway. She finished tightening her boot laces, then stood up and hurriedly skipped toward the door, joining the sergeant major. While standing arm in arm, the two of them turned the corner together and entered the dimly lit hallway leading to Room 33.

Phoenix and Nikita heard the door shut as Dr. Scott closed it behind him. Phoenix's body tingled with a heightened sense of awareness while Nikita Oleshun fought the urge to escape and run. Neither of them knew exactly what was waiting on the other side, but Phoenix did not fear for his life. He sensed something else unfolding. Something that had been hidden until now.

The sergeant major stopped outside the heavy steel door and looked at Nikita. Her blue eyes searched his.

"You are safe with me." He spoke to her in an authoritative tone as if there was no need to question anything. She closed her eyes and touched his arm as he pushed the door open.

Phoenix and Nikita entered what seemed like a roomful of eyes, as a small gathering of top-secret agents and government officials watched them pass through the door. There were no empty seats at the large conference table, which could seat up to twenty-five people.

Phoenix scanned the faces of the men now facing him and stood in stunned silence as he recognized the face of his friend, Nick Majors. The same friend he had pulled from the rubble at Fort Bragg after the explosion. Neither he nor Finley had ever caught up with Majors after he was transported to the local hospital. In fact, they never heard from him again. And now Majors was in a room at Area 51. Phoenix's thoughts almost escaped his lips. *What the fuck was going on?*

Nikita didn't move an inch as Phoenix continued to scan the left side of the room. Chief of Staff of the United States Army General Gordon R. Sullivan, reportedly now retired from the military, was seated next to Phoenix's closest ally and only trusted friend, Dr. Nathaniel O'Connor. And Dr. Richard Scott, Chief Scientist of Paranormal Studies and Weapons Systems, was standing right next to him.

"Please. Have a seat." Dr. Scott motioned for Nikita and Phoenix to take the two empty chairs at the head of the table.

Phoenix pulled the chairs back and moved aside, allowing Nikita to be seated at the same time he was. He settled into the well-padded roller chair and leaned forward, placing his arms on the table before him. His jawline was tight and his eyes piercing as he made a final sweep around the right side of the table and stopped where he locked eyes with Nick Majors. He cleared his throat and spoke in a tone his friend had heard before. It was a warning tone, and it only came before Phoenix let all hell break loose.

"What the fuck is going on here? Nick?" Majors flinched.

"Seth." Majors tried to remain calm, answering Phoenix with a short acknowledgment.

Dr. Scott tapped the table and hastily spoke up, interrupting the tense exchange. "Sergeant Major, we need to brief you on some information that you are unaware of."

Phoenix rolled his eyes around to the scientist and nodded in agreement. He wasn't omniscient, so it was not uncommon for the supernatural soldier to miss important intel unless he had a reason to tap into it using his abilities.

Phoenix leaned back and began interrogating the scientist without letting him speak. "How did you know I was in the middle of the fucking desert fighting a Russian assassin?" Phoenix had already begun reading their thoughts.

Dr. Scott cleared his throat but hesitated to speak. General Sullivan interjected. "Sergeant Major Phoenix, we've been tracking you since the attack at Fort Bragg. There hasn't been one second of your day that we didn't know your exact location."

Phoenix avoided showing any emotional response, even though he wanted to stare the general down with a hard frown. As he fought the temptation, he turned his eyes up to meet the general's and maintained a respectful gaze. He kept his temperament in check as he waited for him to continue.

"The CIA and the FBI have had a ghost tracking you at random times and in random locations. And your near-death experience in Bosnia was a setup by the Russian government. Your friend here was sent there to gather intel and a DNA sample from you. But she failed. The bombing was an inside job meant to put her close enough to you to get what they needed."

Phoenix stared back. "Sir, I already know this."

"Yes, but over the last few weeks, you discovered HAARP and other highly classified information that we cannot risk exposure of."

Phoenix shook his head in confusion. He zoomed in on his friend, Nick Majors, and invaded his thoughts. He then demanded a straightforward answer from his once-closest friend and new remote-viewing recruit.

"How long have you been a part of this program?"

Majors tensed up. "Since I got out of the hospital. They came and questioned me about your abilities and asked how long I had known you. All kinds of questions that I wasn't sure how to answer."

"And you were offered an opportunity just like that to be in the Star Gate program?"

"No. They tested me just like they did Finley. But I tested strongly in remote viewing. I could see things, Seth. And I was damn good at it." Majors emphasized his words with an awestruck tone.

"So, it's been you following me all along?" Phoenix asked his friend, who now looked down at the table.

"Yes, I saw the Russian, and I knew exactly when and where that bastard was going to ambush you. It was me who sent out the alert and got the choppers in the air."

The room was dead silent as Phoenix processed his friend's confession. He offered Nick Majors an appreciative look but declined a verbal response.

Dr. Richard Scott then spoke, breaking the silence. "We have a proposition for you, Phoenix."

Phoenix shifted into his chair. He felt a sense of dread, and Nikita responded in a like fashion as she noticed a change in the scientist's tone.

"We saved Ms. Oleshun from becoming dog food. Without our help, she will not survive. The Russians will hunt her down, but we have approval from the White House to offer her full asylum and a new identity in the United States." Dr. Scott glanced over at Nikita, then back at Phoenix.

Phoenix's eyes narrowed as he studied Dr. Scott. "What do you want?" His tone was forceful, but then in one swift motion, Phoenix put his hand out in front of him, palm facing outward.

"No, wait. I'm done. I want out. I've done my time." He shook his head as he spoke.

Dr. Scott turned and looked at Dr. O'Connor, who sat with his chin resting in his hand. O'Connor declined to speak. Dr. Scott turned back to Phoenix. He spoke with a firm and unrelenting tone as he ordered the sergeant major to kill on command.

"We want you to kill. As you are ordered to do so. You are a soldier, Phoenix. A soldier for the United States of America."

Phoenix leaned back in his chair. A sickening pain stabbed Nikita in the stomach, causing her to gasp.

Phoenix stared in disbelief. He had seen enough death and now only wanted to use his extraordinary capabilities for good. He didn't want to be anybody's assassin. He wanted to go home.

"No," Phoenix spoke with calmness, yet his tone left little to discern. He was stern. His decision was non-negotiable.

The scientist looked at him with a sideways smile and responded. "Sergeant Major, we trained you. We made you who you are. If you don't do what we ask, we can make sure you don't live to see daylight."

Phoenix jumped up and slammed his fists against the table as he leaned forward, almost touching the scientist's nose with his own.

"Don't you ever threaten me, you son of a bitch! If I can stop another man's heart from beating, what the fuck makes you think that I can't stop yours?"

Dr. Scott felt Phoenix's breath against his face and backed off.

Dr. O'Connor stood up and motioned for the sergeant major to relax. He spoke to Phoenix in a fatherly tone.

"Seth, your friend will die if she leaves this area anytime soon. With both of you heading up the remote viewing programs here, we can stop terrorism before it strikes the homeland."

Phoenix slowed his breathing and moved away from Dr. Scott. He refused to sit back down but remained standing at the head of the table. He looked down at Nikita, who sat quietly, not daring to show emotion or incite any reactions aimed in her direction. She was scared. Beyond the walls that separated them from the outside, she could see the end for her and Phoenix as dozens of armed guards waited to rip them to shreds if they resisted. In this moment, she feared everything and everybody. Except for Seth Phoenix.

"The Russian government thinks she's dead?" Phoenix posed a necessary reality for her survival as a question.

"We'll make sure that's the story the Russians hear from the ambassador."

Phoenix nodded once before informing the men inside Room 33 of his final offer. He wasn't backing off, and he didn't give a damn if he had to squeeze the life out of everybody in the room.

"Gentlemen, when I walk out that door, I want to be a free man. I refuse to be a test tube for the mad scientists of the U.S. military, and I'm damn sure not going to let you clone me into some degenerate killing machine. Do you understand?" Phoenix paused. He scanned the faces of every person at the table. Then he continued.

"Give me a place here, and I will work for the country that I have served with honor and integrity. I'm willing to do contract work for the military. I'll be your secret agent, and I'll work with Dr. O'Connor here as I always have. He's been with me since this circus started months ago. I'll help defend the homeland with Nikita Oleshun by my side, but only under those conditions. Otherwise, I'm walking out of here, and I fucking dare you to try and stop me." Phoenix glared at the scientist.

Dr. Scott turned to Dr. O'Connor, who was now fighting to hide a sense of victory on his face.

Dr. O'Connor responded to Phoenix with a nod and then spoke. "Sergeant Major, I believe that's fair. As you know, I've headed some of these programs for the past decade, and my research can't move forward without you and Ms. Oleshun on the team."

Phoenix nodded in agreement with the doctor's offer. He then reached down and took Nikita Oleshun's hand, lifting her out of the chair and onto her feet. He turned to Dr. Scott as he reached for the door.

"You can call off your watchdogs now because I'm getting the hell out of here for a few days."

Dr. O'Connor spoke in a panicked voice. "Where are you going?"

Phoenix stopped at the door and glanced back over his shoulder. "To see Abigail and Stephen Phoenix."

Dr. Scott looked at Dr. O'Connor with an inquisitive stare.

Dr. O'Connor answered the scientist's inquisitive look. "Chattanooga."

The door slowly shut behind them as Nikita Oleshun followed Phoenix out the door. She looked bewildered as she repeated Dr. O'Connor's words in a broken pronunciation. "Chatta--noo--ga?"

Phoenix laughed. "Yeah, Chattanooga."

Nikita smiled and asked. "Where is this place?"

Phoenix turned and admired her features, absorbing her beauty for a moment. Then he reached for her hand and locked his fingers in hers as they walked toward a red exit sign at the end of the hall.

"Home." The sergeant major affirmed.

L. Sydney Fisher

The

PHOENIX

Report

Fact versus Fiction

The Phoenix Project

About four years ago, while I was studying psychic phenomena and psychic development in humans, I stumbled upon a book by Major Ed Dames titled *Tell Me What You See*. I was immediately drawn in by the author's claims that our military had been running a psychic spy program for the last two decades. Reading the book led me to more questions and a Pandora's box whose seal should never be broken. But unrelenting curiosity led me to spend the next two years reading everything I could get my hands on about the clandestine Star Gate program. Two years later, Sergeant Major Seth Phoenix was born of research that uncovered a real-life psychic/telekinetic living in Russia during the Star Gate era, ultimately inspiring the creation of *The Phoenix Series*.

During the course of research for this book project, I studied a number of subjects, locations, and phenomena. Of most significance to me was the content on psychic development in humans and the genetic factors involved. During the Star Gate program, soldiers were trained to be psychic spies by using a method called remote viewing. I was later informed that remote viewing could be taught to anyone, but the military's real interest was in individuals who scored highly on tests of psychic abilities such as clairvoyance and ESP.

The Star Gate program was in operation for more than two decades and consumed a twenty-million-dollar budget by the time it was terminated in November 1995. The U.S. Army's top remote viewers were consulted to help locate missing children and criminals, as well as spy on foreign governments. The program was also reportedly used to locate American hostages taken by a group of Iranians who took over the U.S. Embassy in Tehran from November 4, 1979, to January 20, 1981. While the Clinton Administration has been noted for shutting down the Star

Gate program, the top-secret operation was actually born in 1975 and received support from three presidents, most notably Ronald Reagan.

On March 2, 1990, Tom Clancy's *The Hunt for Red October* was released in movie theatres all across America. The film told the story of a Russian submarine captain wishing to defect. The Typhoon-class nuclear missile sub was actually based on a real-life vessel the Russians had been building for some time. U. S. Army Remote Viewer 001, Joseph McMoneagle, has been credited with discovering the Russian submarine's manufacturing point during a remote viewing session.

Star Gate was conducted at Fort Meade, Maryland, in a wood-frame shed that served as the base headquarters. The program was highly classified, with only about one hundred people supposedly aware of its existence. All remote viewers were required to sign an oath of absolute secrecy. Any breach of their contract could result in a $10,000 fine and possible jail time.

These paranormal studies were also being conducted by the military and in association with the Stanford Research Institute, located in California. SRI was once affiliated with Stanford University until it became a separate entity in 1970. As a non-profit research institute, it was dedicated to client-sponsored research and development, including the U.S. Army's remote viewing program.

By September 1995, the CIA had already ceased all remote viewing work, and all staff members had been reassigned elsewhere. At the end of the CIA's review of the Star Gate program and its real contribution to the military, it was decided that the project had not offered significant findings and would therefore be terminated by November. Opponents to the program's shutdown argued that the assessment took less than two months to review over twenty-three years of research. And of the thousands of sessions conducted, only ten experiments of the last twelve months of operation were studied. In other words, only one percent of the program's total available data was considered in the review.

After Star Gate's official termination, some staff members commented that the program had ended for several reasons, most notably a lack of support within the military and intel, poor management, and, lastly, the media's growing scrutiny. Others still believe today that the United States is secretly operating the Star Gate program.

Another military-based research project of paranormal interest to me was the HAARP program located near Gakona, Alaska. Work on the HAARP (High Frequency Active Auroral Research Program) began in 1993 and was led by the United States Air Force, the United States Navy, the Defense Advanced Research Projects Agency, and the University of Alaska Fairbanks. The program's research focuses on the ionosphere and its response to the sun. The research was intended to benefit the military's communication and navigational systems. The program was said to have successfully developed better communication methods for submarines. But despite the program's declarations, conspiracy theories have abounded.

According to many conspiracy theorists, HAARP is nothing more than a machine developed by the United States to control the weather and use it as a weapon. Some theorists blame HAARP for global warming, earthquakes, tornadoes, and hurricanes. And it has been said that HAARP is an instrument used for mind control. While these theories have never been proven, the program was officially shut down by the United States Air Force in 2014, but the University of Alaska assumed ownership of the program and its facility by August 2015. At the time of this writing (April 2017), the program is reportedly officially back up and running.

While setting up the story outline for *The Phoenix Series,* I investigated psychic phenomena known as telekinesis and extrasensory perception (ESP). As a believer, my research was not aimed at debunking the supernatural but, more importantly, at understanding it. If telekinesis were a real and natural occurrence among certain individuals, what was causing it to happen? And one more question. Why are some people more psychic than others?

Reports of psychic abilities, telepathic communication, and supernatural phenomena such as telekinesis have been noted for centuries. In fact, some statistics suggest that more than fifty percent of Americans believe in the paranormal and the supernatural, such as miracles or angelic appearances. During my analysis of psychic individuals, I noticed a few parallels that coincided with some of the information I had studied. In one of the books I read about psychic children (The Children of Now), it stated that a common denominator among psychic people was blue eyes. And after examining pictures of the remote viewers in the Star Gate program, I noticed that the top four appeared to have blue eyes.

> Major Ed Dames—Blue Eyes
> Joseph McMoneagle—Blue Eyes
> Ingo Swann—Blue Eyes
> Lyn Buchanan—Blue Eyes
> David Morehouse—Unable to verify.

I then decided to look at other famous psychics to see if they shared the same traits. I searched for famous individuals who claimed to possess psychic or supernatural abilities. One of the most convincing was Jeanne Dixon, the astrologer and psychic who reportedly had a dream of John F. Kennedy's assassination prior to the event. She even called the White House and asked the president *not* to go to Dallas. And the color of her eyes? She was a blue-eyed beauty with red hair. So, does this mean that a brown-eyed person cannot be psychic? Of course not. But the parallels are there and worth consideration.

In other references, I found medical research that explained how psychics often share the same characteristics, such as being ambidextrous. And they often report that someone in their immediate family either has the "gift" of insight now, or it may have been present in a now-deceased relative. Could this suggest that "psychic gifts" are genetic?

Other noted traits of the psychic sometimes involved a near-death encounter and/or an out-of-body experience, known as a Near Death Experience (NDE). The individual often reported a spike in their abilities after surviving a near-fatal event. Science has attempted to explain the NDE as a hallucination experienced due to a lack of oxygen. However, there are literally millions of people who have experienced NDE's and the similarities of their stories are too uncanny to dismiss.

The final part of this project's research landed me in the middle of Nina Kulagina's biography. Born on July 30, 1926, the Russian psychic and telekinetic served in the Russian army at the young age of fourteen. She reportedly could move objects at will and was said to possess healing abilities. She was studied by dozens of scientists and became an international name when she demonstrated the ability to stop a frog's heart during a scientific experiment held on March 10, 1970.

Nina Kulagina was the inspiration for Nikita Oleshun's character in *The Phoenix Series*. The small-framed, brown-eyed woman was married to a Russian engineer and had three children. She sustained a battle injury to the abdomen that caused chronic pain for most of her life. In her later years, it was stated that her abilities had faded, possibly due to aging, chronic pain from the battle wound, and the effects of childbirth. She died on April 11, 1990, from a heart attack. She was 63 years old.

In conclusion, writing *The Phoenix Series* has been exciting. I will miss the sergeant major and his Russian friend, Nikita. However, my research into unexplained mysteries will never cease. Having experienced an NDE at the age of fifteen and witnessing too many paranormal encounters to list, I will remain a believer in the possibility of supernatural phenomena. And it isn't a coincidence that you are reading this report, because in a world of infinite possibilities, there is no such thing as accidents. Just remember, in the end, and by direct orders of the CIA, this never happened.

Until we meet again,

L. Sydney Fisher

Who is the fictional SETH PHOENIX?

Name: Seth Phoenix
Call name: Seth
Age: 39
Birthdate: March 21, 1956 (Born on the cusp of Pisces and Aries)
Place of birth: Chattanooga, Tennessee
Height: 6'3"
Weight: 210 lbs.
Eye color: Intense blue
Hair color: Dark Brown
Distinguishing marks: A star-shaped birthmark near his temple and hidden inside his hairline.
Special notes about Seth: He was born a star child. Possesses the ability of clairvoyance, telepathy, and telekinesis. Anger causes his energy to dissipate and become chaotic, leading to the destruction of nearby objects and the displacement of material things.
Father's name: Stephen Phoenix
Father's current status: Living
Mother's name: Abigail Phoenix
Current status: Living
Ethnic background: White/Cherokee Indian. German/Irish
Religion: Protestant
Degree of religious practice: Very spiritual but doesn't attend church regularly.
Marital status: Never married
Children: None
Police Record: None
Medical Record: Excellent. No pre-existing conditions.

Who is the factual NIKITA OLESHUN?

Name: Ninel Sergeyevna Kulagina
Call name: Nina
Age: 63 at death
Birthdate: July 30, 1926
Died: April 11, 1990
Cause: Heart Attack
Place of birth: St. Petersburg (Leningrad), Russia
Height: 5'1"
Weight: 110 lbs.
Eye color: Brown
Hair color: Dark Brown
Special notes about Nina: The former Russian Sergeant claimed she first recognized her abilities in her youth and believed she inherited them from her mother. According to Kulagina, she noticed her telekinetic abilities when items spontaneously moved around her when she was angry. She also reported that in order to manifest the effect, she required a period of meditation and a clear mind void of any interference. Upon reaching the required focus for the phenomena, she is said to have experienced sharp pain in her spine and blurred eyesight. Reportedly, storms were known to interfere with her ability to perform psychokinetic acts.
Religion: Unknown
Marital status: Married to Viktor Vasilievich Kulagina, a Russian naval engineer
Children: Three
Medical Record: Suffered a battle wound to the abdomen at age 17. (January 1944) She underwent five operations but endured chronic pain for the rest of her life.

SUGGESTED READING

Dames, Major Ed. and Newman, Joel Harry (2011).
Tell Me What You See. Hoboken, New Jersey:
John Wiley & Sons, Inc.

McMoneagle, Joseph (2000). *Remote Viewing
Secrets: A Handbook*. Charlottesville, Virginia:
Hampton Roads Publishing Company, Inc.

Losey, Meg Blackburn, MSC.D, PH.D. (2007).
The Children of Now. Franklin Lakes, NJ: New
Page Books.

Morehouse, David (1996). *Psychic Warrior*.
New York, NY: St. Martin's Press.

Buchanan, Lyn (2003). *The Seventh Sense: The
Secrets of Remote Viewing as Told By a Psychic
Spy for the U.S. Military*. New York, NY: Pocket
Books, a division of Simon & Schuster, Inc.

Ritchey, David (2003). *The H.I.S.S. of the A.S.P.:
Understanding the Anomalously Sensitive
Person*. Terra Alta, West Virginia: Headline
Books, Inc.

HAVE YOU HEARD ABOUT THIS STORY?

A PREVIEW of *See No Evil*

Chapter 1

Missionary Ridge. Chattanooga, Tennessee
November 25, 1863
3:00 p.m.

The sound of footsteps sliding across the grassy slope alerted the Rebel forces of an impending attack as the Federals charged up the side of the mountain, their boots heavy and marred with mud formed from the recent rain. As they pushed forward into Confederate territory, they began to shout, their roars echoing across the side of the ridge.

"Chickamauga! Chickamauga!" The Federals chanted in unison.

Confederate General Braxton Bragg stared into the face of certain victory, his deep brown eyes moistened by the chilling blast that swept over his face and caused him to step backward. It was a warning; a cold harbinger alerting him of the end as he quickly began to order his men's retreat. But the order came too late as the federal troops advanced. The Yankees had begun to charge the ridge without the order from Union General Thomas George. They had taken the advance under their own promissory and burst forth with a force so powerful that thousands of men fell to their deaths. Haunting screams could be heard as bodies tumbled hundreds of feet down the hillside, while others found their graves where they fell.

Blood splattered in every direction as bullets split skulls and severed carotid arteries. The bloody death found its mark upon the hands of some of the men still standing who, in a desperate attempt to save their best friend's life, dragged the lifeless body until their own need to survive forced them into abandonment.

Thomas Jefferson Brown, 34th Alabama Infantry Regiment, Company B, fell to his knees. He grimaced in pain as his kneecaps hit the rocky slag surface. His feet cramped inside his boots, and his arms trembled from fatigue. He held his musket tight, his head lowered, and his eyes closed as he felt the enemy's encirclement.

Just as the enemy's shouts rang loud, he felt a quick, hard thrust from the bottom of a boot. The Yankee kicked him breathless and sent his body forward as he slammed face-first into the rock. The tender skin of his left brow split open and began to bleed, the blood trickling into his eye socket.

"Get up, Soldier. Get up and fight." The Yankee mocked him and attempted to roll his body over with his foot.

Thomas Jefferson Brown was not near death, but he might as well have been. He was now a captured Confederate soldier and a prisoner of war to the Federals. Seconds seemed like hours as his mind played back the conversation that he had with his best friend, Lewis Meadow Prater, who was serving with him. Both men had enlisted in Coosa County, Alabama. The regiment was organized on April 15, 1862, and then moved to Tupelo, Mississippi, and was placed under General Arthur M. Manigault's Brigade.

Prater and Brown had it made in Tupelo. The camp was well-guarded, and food was plentiful. They were positioned on the east side in a Confederate camp that housed several hundred men overlooking the city. It was on this hillside where Prater and Brown ate their evening supper of corn, salt pork, and bread while sitting around the glowing campfires that could be seen almost a mile away near General Bragg's headquarters. The Tupelo camps were part of what became known as the "Black Prairie" for its fertile land. Crops were easily grown in abundance, and livestock were plentiful. Thus, Tupelo and its region were capable of feeding the entire Confederate Army of the West.

On the evening before Prater and Brown were set to depart for Chattanooga, Brown unknowingly revealed a man's destiny. During the evening meal, he nudged his friend, Lewis Prater, while both men finished the last of their bread rations.

"Lewis, my good friend, I have an urgent request of you and beg for your consent." Thomas Jefferson Brown locked eyes with his closest friend as he thought of his wife back in Coosa County, Alabama. What would happen to Martha if she became a widow? How would she raise their two sons alone? Prater was his first consideration. Although Prater was nineteen years old, he had never married and had no children.

Prater looked intently at Brown as he broke a piece of bread. "Yes, of course. What is it?"

Brown looked away and hesitated for a brief moment as he collected his thoughts, then glanced back at Prater. "I need you to promise to take care of Martha if I'm killed. I need you to promise me that you'll do it. Please. She'll be raising my sons alone. You aren't married, and it would be an honor for me."

Prater's eyes moistened as he stared into the eyes of his best friend and considered the reality that one of them might be killed within a few days. Would this be the last meal that he had with his best friend?

Prater accepted the bread that Brown passed to him. The reality of war was upon them. "I'm honored by your request. I pray that we both come home, but I will promise to take care of your family if something happens to you. You have my word." Prater stood up, and Brown joined him in front of the campfire as the two men embraced. Tears moistened the eyes of the best friends. Then Brown pulled back and looked Prater in the eyes. His hands were now clasped together as if he were about to pray. "Thank you. Thank you, my friend."

Brown's mind quickly snapped back to the present as he felt his hands bound with a leather strap. The leather stung as it was tightened around his wrists, almost cutting off the circulation. Two men hoisted him to his feet and shoved him forward, forcing him to walk down the hill where he would join over 5,000 other Confederates now destined for Rock Island, Illinois.

Chapter 2

Thomas Jefferson Brown climbed into the railcar as the other prisoners waited for boarding. Although the train was destined for the three-mile-long Mississippi River Island known as Rock Island, Illinois, it would take several days to arrive as a few hundred at a time poured into the camp. And by January 9th, 1864, just a few weeks after the Union victory at Missionary Ridge, all 6,158 captured Confederates had arrived.

The prison camp had already been notified to expect an influx of prisoners from the battle at Missionary Ridge. On November 24, just one day before the battle, a guard assigned at the prison reported that he had "no blankets, no record book, no water in the prison yard, or clothing of any kind for the Confederates". And yet the prisoners were still boarded onto the railcars and transported to what would become for many their final destination.

Brown sat cramped in the middle of dozens of other soldiers piled almost on top of each other in the railcar. Although the conditions were not comfortable, the dozens of men cramped together generated enough body heat to help alleviate some of the bitter cold that seeped through the cracks in the railcar's door. And as the train traveled farther north, crossing Indiana and much of Illinois, the train's lonely whistle faded into the sound of the howling wind as it slapped against the outside railcar's wall.

Brown's stomach churned and ached from lack of food, and he was becoming dehydrated. The cut above his left brow had finally ceased bleeding, but the stinging pain lingered as tiny pebbles of dirt and rock covered the open wound.

His mind drifted back to the battlefield. He remembered seeing the coattail of General Braxton Bragg at a distance as he narrowly escaped capture and certain death. The general's 5'10" slender frame faded into the background of his army's dead or captured men that now scattered the landscape. Brown remembered the general overseeing the camps in Tupelo, the headquarters of the Confederate Army of the West, where he had spent the last several months before the day came when Bragg sent word to General Manigault that his brigade would depart by train the following day for Chattanooga, Tennessee. He now longed to feel the warmth of his wife's touch, but his heart had known since the day he left Alabama that he might never see those comforts again, and Tupelo might become the only remaining semblance of home.

Hours turned into days as the train passed through depots heavily lined with young recruits waiting to replenish the Union army. The men's morale hit an all-time low as the reality of their demise became certain. The "Cause" was undoubtedly hopeless as they contemplated a war that never seemed to end.

The train's wheels squealed against the steel rails as it came to a halt near the prison camp. The heavy steel doors slid open, exposing daylight and mounds of glittering white powder that reflected the sun's light against a backdrop of ice-laden trees. The men's eyes were squinting as they emptied the boxcar, falling into snow two feet deep.

Brown struggled to put one foot in front of the other as he started the fourth of a mile trek toward the prison camp. Of the four hundred plus men that arrived with him, dozens of them found themselves barefoot in knee-deep snow and fighting temperatures unlike anything they had ever experienced in the South's steamy climate. It was a different kind of hell. A hell where freezing to death or suffering frostbite to the feet was a common occurrence. With no blankets or clothing for Confederate soldiers who were already thinly clad, there was little hope of survival.

Brown finally reached the barracks, which typically held 120 men, with three tiers of bunks. With the temperature registering just above freezing at 35 degrees Fahrenheit, Brown was shivering so violently that he could barely stand on two feet. He stumbled inside the building, hardly equipped to house hundreds of soldiers. The roof was all that separated the men from the night sky and the falling snow. There was no ceiling, and little protection against the elements other than the walls that blocked the icy gusts of wind swirling and howling outside.

Brown followed the line of men until he reached the bunk now designated for him. He fell against the bed and curled into a ball as dozens of his Confederate friends did the same. Within minutes, exhaustion overtook his body, and his eyes closed.

By morning, Thomas Jefferson Brown joined the ranks of those who died within the walls of Rock Island, Illinois, prison. Cause of death: exposure. His body lay motionless and hard like a block of ice. His fingers were unable to be pried open from the balled-up fists that he held onto as his hands turned blue and slowly froze solid. The gash on his eye was no longer an open cut, but rather icy and sealed shut with traces of dried blood that had trickled down the side of his left cheek. Thomas Jefferson Brown would not suffer. His end had come fast, unlike many of the others who would spend months fighting disease and freezing temperatures.

Days later, Prater received word of his best friend's death, making him the benefactor of Thomas Jefferson Brown's family, just as he had promised. While Brown's death was tragic, it was this destiny that was paving the way for a boy to be born four years later on April 21st, 1867, in Coosa County, Alabama. Because of his commitment to Thomas Jefferson Brown, Lewis Prater would father a child destined to leave behind a legacy and a gift that only God could understand and the Devil could seek to destroy.

Chapter 3

The Gordon Hotel
January 1880
Aberdeen, Mississippi

Seymour Prater stood outside the majestic red brick hotel located on East Commerce Street in Aberdeen, Mississippi. It had been years since Lewis Prater had married his best friend's widow and fathered a child with her. The couple lived in Alabama for a few years after the War of the States ended and during Reconstruction. They then moved to Monroe County, Mississippi, where the roots of Seymour Prater's supernatural legacy would be planted.

The small southern town of Aberdeen was located on the banks of the Tombigbee River, where explorer Hernando De Soto had once camped. It survived the Civil War with most of its buildings still intact, and the town now boasts a population of over 2,300 people.

Seymour gazed up at the second floor of the hotel, admiring its grandeur. It was the finest hotel along the Tombigbee Riverbanks in North Mississippi. And it served the area well since Aberdeen was one of Mississippi's busiest ports in the land where cotton was king.

He put one foot onto the front walkway leading into the hotel and stopped. He quickly leaned back just in time to avoid being hit in the face as the door swung open. Patrons of the hotel, one right after another, followed past the open door to the horses and buggies that lined the front outside entrance. Seymour watched as three, then five, men dressed in charcoal gray, pinstripe suits and matching top hats exited the hotel. As the last man stepped forward through the doorway, Seymour rushed inside, letting the door swing back against him.

John Davenport, Captain of the Tombigbee River boat *Johnson*, stepped inside The Gordon Hotel for the first time since its opening day. The interior first floor was bustling with shoppers and patrons visiting the hotel for a haircut in the barbershop or to browse the various merchant shops, where they might purchase a fine, tailored gentleman's suit or a handcrafted leather hat and matching shoes, now affordable thanks to their recent cotton trade. But Davenport's mood was heavily laden with doubt and anxiety as he mulled over an uncertain future since preparing for his final voyage down the Tombigbee River. He had been enlisted to oversee the Hargrove's estate for the past few years, transporting cotton when the river water levels allowed. Today, the riverboat was forced to dock overnight as the river's water level registered just below the ten-foot depths that were considered safe for travel to Columbus, Mississippi. With overcast skies and heavy rain expected by nightfall, the trip would most likely become navigable by mid-morning.

Davenport lifted his hat and raked strands of hair away from his eyes. He pushed the hat back down, fitting it against his head, and stood still with one hand on his hip as he glanced around the giant open area of the first floor. His eyes circled the room as he admired the decorative grandeur. The hotel's front desk was lined with guests checking into the area's newest and finest lodging place along the upper Tombigbee River. Hundreds of passengers from the many Tombigbee Riverboats had already visited the hotel within weeks of its "Open for Business" announcement. The hotel had been made possible by investors, who promised its tenants a prosperous future. Among the many occupants were entrepreneurs such as grocers, clothing merchants, barbershops, and the local newspaper, The Aberdeen Weekly.

Davenport walked to a nearby sitting area decorated with fancy, carved wooden chairs upholstered in plush red velvet cushions. He sat down and examined his boots that were covered with dust from the nearby street. He was in the wrong place. The hotel and the likes of it were much too fancy for him and his blood. He was a riverboat captain who spent many years sleeping in a bunk barely equipped to house his tall, large frame. He was used to uncomfortable conditions, and it was a life that he had become accustomed to. The scenic route along the flowing riverbanks was a pristine setting where raccoons played, deer roamed, and the occasional glimpse of a panther climbing a low-hanging tree branch sent a rapid heartbeat as it locked eyes with Davenport.

His heart was on the Tombigbee River, and the thought of this being his last trip for Mr. W. H. Hargrove caused him much grief since the railroad would now be the main means of transportation for Hargrove's cotton. Would his riverboat find more work, possibly transporting other goods to the area or even as far south as Mobile?

The young Seymour Prater watched people come and go from a corner of the hotel lobby where he positioned himself away from the traffic and inquisitive eyes of the hotel staff. He was a quiet kid with a curious nature who rarely missed an opportunity to help someone or offer advice that seemed well beyond his youthful years. He had never understood his bizarre ability to "see" into the nature of others and even determine their destinies through mental pictures that played out in his mind. And he had never told anybody about his uncanny gift for fear of ridicule or disbelief. It was an oddity that he endured alone, except when he "felt" the need to share an insight that could not be withheld within his good conscience.

Seymour watched through the storefront window as his mother shopped in one of the grocery markets inside the hotel. Martha Prater savored the smell of fresh bread as she quickly lifted it to her nose before placing it into her basket. She joined dozens of other women this morning, eager to shop among the hotel's many venues, and she had allowed Seymour to accompany her to the hotel since she would most likely need his assistance to carry her bags.

An invisible prompt suddenly caused Seymour to look away and turn his eyes toward John Davenport, sitting in a chair across the room. He studied the man's expression and the way his body leaned forward in the chair, not sitting all the way back. He watched as the man studied his own feet. He noticed him bend over and down as he wiped his first two fingers across the toe of his boot before examining the rug beneath his feet.

Seymour's uncanny gift of insight came alive at that moment as he received the man's thoughts as invisible messages. It was as if he was plugging into a radio frequency that only John Davenport could hear, yet Seymour was an unknown invader who, regardless of his harmless intent, could no longer control his own inclinations to see into the lives of others than he could control his body's natural urges of hunger or excretion.

Davenport's anxiety was real. He thought about the possibility of the railroad now taking over as a main means of transport. He knew that his security had been threatened. And while Davenport's thoughts filled the rafters of his mind, Seymour Prater listened in as the static became clearer. What would he do with the last two decades of his life now gone? He was a river captain, and John Davenport could not conceive of any other identity.

Seymour watched Davenport and sensed a need to address him. Flashes of insight in the form of pictures now flooded his mind. He became compelled to walk across the room and sit in the chair opposite and facing Davenport. Seymour ran his hands over the plush velvet seat of the chair, feeling its soft texture and admiring how the scarlet color seemed to shift as he brushed his fingers back and forth.

Davenport glanced over at the young man sitting across from him and watched him with the same curiosity that had led Seymour across the room. What had brought the kid into the hotel lobby? Was he a runaway? Davenport studied the youth's demeanor for a few seconds before greeting him.

Davenport nodded and spoke in an even, friendly tone. "Good morning, young man. What brings you to this fine hotel?"

The corners of Seymour's mouth turned upward into a friendly smile. "Good Morning, Sir. This is my first visit to the hotel since it opened. I'm just waiting here for my mama while she shops." Seymour pointed toward one of the hotel storefronts.

"Ah, ok." Davenport nodded.

"You're a river captain, aren't you?" Seymour's inquisitive nature took over, relinquishing his otherwise shy disposition.

Davenport watched the boy's face. There was something odd about him in an uncanny kind of way. He looked to be about eleven years old, but his mannerisms, like the way he rubbed his eyes when he talked and the way he turned his head before he spoke, echoed the body language of someone much older. Like an elderly man. Yes, he reminded Davenport of an old man.

"Yes, I am. I've been a riverboat captain—

"For over twenty years. Your home is on the river." Seymour interrupted, finishing his sentence. He paused and then continued to disclose glimpses of the mental images he had witnessed a few moments earlier.

"I saw you on the riverboat *Johnson*. You work for Mr. Hargrove, but you're scared that you won't have a job in a few months when he starts using the railroad. Don't worry." Seymour paused as Davenport stared in disbelief.

"Who are you, Kid? How do you know this?" Davenport leaned back in his seat and took a deep breath.

"I'm nobody, Sir. I just have some sort of odd talent, I guess." Seymour looked away and studied his hands folded in his lap.

"What do you mean that you 'saw me on the riverboat Johnson'?" Davenport was quickly forming an opinion about the boy, but he had questions of his own.

"Oh, I just meant that I saw you in my mind. That's all." Seymour rubbed his fingers across his brow.

"You saw me in your mind? Can you see other things?" Davenport was now intrigued. He was well aware of Seymour's rare natural talent. He had only known one other person in his lifetime with the 'gift', but the former slave girl who lived on the Hargrove Plantation had been dead for years. Before being stricken with Typhoid Fever, she was considered to be Hargrove's most prized possession and often advised Master Hargrove of unseen troubles on the horizon. He had witnessed the supernatural wonders of her insights many times, and she had confided in Hargrove and Davenport, who were often by his side more than anyone else in his circle. Davenport knew how she kept her abilities sharp. He knew what she was doing each morning before sunrise when she left the cabin and walked twenty feet to the old tree stump overshadowed by hanging vines and honeysuckle blooms. He had seen her sitting there with her eyes closed, not saying a word. Just still and quiet for several minutes until it was time to return to the morning's work at the plantation mansion.

"Yes, Sir. I see pictures. Not all the time, but I started seeing pictures of you almost as soon as you entered the hotel. And I knew that I should tell you not to worry." Seymour spoke barely above a whisper as people passed near them on their way to the hotel's front check-in counter.

Davenport sighed with relief and lifted his hat as he combed his hair back once again before standing to leave the hotel. He looked at the youth now standing before him in the hotel lobby. Seymour Prater had given him an important and timely message. He had offered encouragement and hope. And now Davenport knew that he must instruct Seymour Prater about the reality of his visions. He must instruct him to develop his abilities.

"What's your name, Kid?" Davenport reached out and patted Seymour on the shoulder.

"Seymour. Seymour Prater, Sir."

"Well, my good man, Seymour, it wasn't an accident that our paths crossed today. You understand that, don't you?" Davenport looked hard and straight in Seymour's eyes.

"Yes, Sir. I believe so."

"Good. Then here's what you need to do from this day forward and for the rest of your life. You must develop this special gift that you have. It will be your calling in life. You understand?"

Seymour nodded. "Yes, but I don't know how."

Davenport motioned for Seymour to step aside as hotel guests began to take the now-empty seats that they had vacated. They took a few steps forward and stopped near the hotel's front door.

Davenport spoke clearly. "You must learn how to clear your mind and focus, Young Man. It's called meditation. You must practice this for a few minutes every day. It will open channels to you. First, find a quiet place to be alone and focus on a question in your mind, then be quiet and wait."

Seymour nodded in spite of the slight bit of confusion that he was feeling. He repeated Davenport's instructions. "Focus and clear my mind."

"Yes, that's right. I've only known one other person who could do it. And you will get better at it as time goes by. Now I have to get going. You do what I told you." Davenport patted Seymour once again on the back and reached for the door handle.

Seymour stood still in the doorway as he paused and watched John Davenport walk out ahead of him. Davenport looked back over his shoulder one last time and nodded as he spoke. "Focus. Good luck, young man." He turned the corner at the north end of the hotel and faded out of sight.

It would be the first and last time that Seymour ever saw John Davenport, but this chance meeting and Davenport's instructions would prove to be the most important guidance that he would ever receive. Davenport's timely message had set the stage for the beginning of what would become a supernatural legacy destined to be delivered by none other than Seymour R. Prater.

To get the rest of this story and other books by this author, please visit...

LSYDNEYFISHER.COM

HAVE YOU HEARD ABOUT THIS STORY?

Dear Reader,

If you enjoyed this book, please consider leaving a review. Reviews are valuable to authors, and we appreciate hearing from you!

I hope you will join me again on another supernatural adventure.

Until then,

L. Sydney Fisher

www.ingramcontent.com/pod-product-compliance
Lightning Source LLC
Chambersburg PA
CBHW030424290526
45786CB00001B/133